HEARING
THE SPIRIT

CHRISTOPHER ASH

HEARING
THE SPIRIT

Knowing the Father through the Son

PTRESOURCES

CHRISTIAN
FOCUS

Copyright © Christopher Ash 2011

paperback – ISBN 978-1-84550-725-1
epub – ISBN 978-1-84550-991-0
mobi – ISBN 978-1-84550-768-8

10 9 8 7 6 5 4 3

Published in 2011, reprinted in 2015
This edition reprinted in 2017
with Truth for Life
P.O. Box 398000, Cleveland, Ohio 44139, U.S.A.
by Christian Focus Publications,
Geanies House, Fearn, Tain, Ross-shire,
IV20 1TW, Scotland, U.K.
www.christianfocus.com
and
Proclamation Trust Resources,
Willcox House, 140-148 Borough High Street,
London, SE1 1LB, England, Great Britain.
www.proctrust.org.uk

Cover design Moose77.com

Printed in the U.S.A.

Contents

Introduction:

Making the Father known

This book is for anyone who is thirsty for a deep experience of the Spirit of God, who will not be satisfied by anything less than a full, lasting and authentic drinking from the life-giving waters of God Himself. It is about the Spirit of God and His relationship to the Word of God – Jesus the Eternal Word, but particularly the Bible as the written word. It is not about healings, miracles, speaking in tongues or other – sometimes controversial – subjects associated with the Spirit. It is very specifically about the relationship between the Spirit and the Bible.

FOUR CAUSES OF CONCERN

At some stage in their lives most, if not all, Christians are concerned, even anxious, about how the Spirit of God relates to the Bible. There are at least four reasons for this.

Personal anxiety

Soon after God brought me to a living faith in Christ, I met another equally young Christian and told him what had happened to me. 'That's good,' he said, 'but you need to realise that it's nothing compared to what the Spirit has done in my life'. He went on to tell me about some wonderful experience he had had since he first came to faith in Christ. The details are not important. But it seemed unrelated to the Bible. And it unsettled me. I worried that I might be missing out. Perhaps I was. He certainly thought I was.

We are especially prone to this anxiety, if we have been brought up as 'Bible Christians' with a strong emphasis on the centrality of the Bible in our churches and our Christian lives. Is there something more we are missing by focusing so much on the Bible? How does a living experience of the Spirit relate to our sometimes humdrum and pedestrian experience of reading or hearing the Bible? Surely there must be something more. There is, but I don't think it was what my friend was talking about. It is what this book is about.

Devotional longing

Anxiety that we are missing out is a negative emotion. But that can easily turn into something more positive, as we begin to long, thirst and hunger for more of God. I think of times in my Christian life when I have felt, as I often continue to feel, dry. And I long not to feel dry. I want to echo the Bible singer who cries out, 'my soul thirsts for you …in a dry and weary land where there is no water' (Ps. 63:1). But how often is our thirst satisfied? From time to time I am deeply moved, even to tears, under the preaching of the Bible. But how often do you and I come to the Bible dry, and feel that we leave even drier? A young Christian spoke to me recently of how he longed for more reality in his walk with Jesus. The poet and hymn-writer William Cowper, in one of his many periods of depression, wrote in his hymn, 'Oh, for a closer walk with God',

> 'Where is the blessedness I knew when first I saw the Lord?
> Where is the soul-refreshing view of Jesus and his word?'

Or perhaps we sing of Jesus in William Gadsby's great hymn, 'Immortal Honours',

Introduction

'O that my soul could love and praise him more,
His beauties trace, His majesty adore,
Live near His heart, rest in His love each day,
Hear His dear voice and all His will obey.'[1]

But how can we 'hear His dear voice' afresh today? What is the right level of expectation in a sinful world, with still sinful hearts? Can I – ought I – to expect and experience more? Is the Bible the right place to go, the only place to go?

Frustrated zeal

Then again, our interest in these questions may be at the level of frustrated Christian zeal. We live in a culture that doesn't care about Jesus. And then perhaps we read the great twentieth-century Welsh preacher Dr Martyn Lloyd-Jones writing about what he termed, 'unction', the felt anointing of the Spirit on a preacher. He is talking about some wonderful words in Paul's first letter to the church in Thessalonica, where Paul says,

> 'our gospel came to you not simply with words, but also with power, with the Holy Spirit and with deep conviction.'
> (1 Thess. 1:5).

Lloyd-Jones suggests there are times when a preacher senses that he is filled with the Spirit, 'clothed with power and authority', with 'an awareness of a power not your own thrilling through the whole of your being, and an indescribable sense of joy' as 'the Spirit is using you, and you are looking on in great enjoyment and astonishment.' And the people, he says, sense this at once; 'they can tell the difference immediately. They are gripped, they become serious, they are convicted, they are moved, they are humbled…'[2]

Whether or not Lloyd-Jones is right to suggest that the preacher can really be sure when God is using him (and many

---

1   Quote from the *Praise* modernisation – *Praise: Psalms, Hymns and Songs for Christian Worship* (Darlington: Praise Trust, 2000) No. 305.

2   D. M. Lloyd-Jones, *Preaching and Preachers* (London: Hodder and Stoughton, 1971) p. 324f

will testify to times of utter felt weakness and inadequacy as the times when God has actually used them), what Lloyd-Jones describes sounds wonderful. How we would love to be like that, whether we are preachers or just trying to talk to our families or neighbours about Jesus. But how often does it happen?

Where do we go with this frustrated zeal? As I go on in the Christian life I am increasingly concerned that this good and natural frustration and zeal leads some to take a wrong turning in their discipleship and Christian service. Feeling the misery of seeming powerlessness, they hear voices calling them onto a different path. There, they are told, in addition to the Bible, there are other living waters to be found, and they need no longer trudge along their present humdrum way. And yet these may be siren voices. What looks like living water from a distance may turn out to be a mirage.

Church discontent

Lastly our concern may be at the level of a general discontent in a local church. A pastor friend of mine faced criticism because some in the church were saying, 'we aren't making space for the Spirit.' One church member said to him that they'd got, 'too much word and not enough Spirit.' Other church leaders may attract flak from the other flank. 'It is all very well having lots of "Spirit",' say their conservative critics, 'but where is the word?'

For church ministers or pastors who call themselves 'conservative (or classical) evangelical' such discontent can fuel our fear that the Spirit has moved away from our ministry or our church. In our waking dreams we see a hand writing 'Ichabod (the glory has departed)' over our church noticeboards.[3] For every one of us prepared, with a cavalier wave of the hand, to dismiss our more charismatic friends as ignorant, immature or just plain wrong, there are ten of us who worry that it is we who are in the wrong. Even those of us who confidently think

---

3   1 Samuel 4:21

of ourselves as 'charismatic' sometimes worry that we are being bypassed by others, left behind by the wind of the Spirit as it blows somewhere else in some new move of God.

So whether it is personal anxiety, devotional longing, frustrated zeal or discontent in church, we need to think carefully about the Spirit and the Bible.

MAKING THE FATHER KNOWN

Some years ago a famous actor wrote, 'I have to admit that my search for a father has been my constant speculation for 50 years.'[4] Those words were written by the actor Alec Guinness, perhaps best known for his portrayal of Obi-Wan Kenobi in the early *Star Wars* films. He won an Oscar for his portrayal of the half-mad Colonel Nicholson in *The Bridge on the River Kwai*. Guinness came from a very sad background. His mother was a high-class prostitute and he never knew who his father was. Our need for a human father, and for a father's approval, echoes our deep spiritual need for the Father God.

I remember visiting an African friend leading a church in Soweto in South Africa. He and his co-pastor were leading a group of 25 men committed to live for Christ. He told me that not one of those 25 had been brought up with a human father. The heavenly Father is not a substitute for a human father, but He is the one to whom all our natural longings point. He is the satisfaction of our deepest human longings and needs.

Preaching during the closing stages of the Second World War, the German pastor and theologian Helmut Thielicke spoke of the happy times in the world as 'like tiny islands in an ocean of blood and tears.' 'The history of the world', he went on to say, 'is a story of war, deeply marked with the hoofprints of the apocalyptic horsemen. It is the story of humanity without a Father – *so it seems*.'[5]

---

4   Quoted in Obituary in *The Week*. (12th August 2000)

5   Helmut Thielicke, *The Prayer that Spans the World: sermons on the Lord's Prayer* (ET London: James Clarke, 1965), p. 21 (his italics)

Hearing the Spirit

Jesus came to make known the Father to men and women in a world of blood and tears. The defining event in the history of the universe was when Jesus of Nazareth made the invisible Father God known. In His prayer to the Father just before He died, these words bracket the main section of Jesus' prayer:

'*I have revealed you…I have made you known.*' (John 17:6, 26)

This revelation or 'making known' was right at the heart of all Jesus did. It was focused first on His apostles. 'I have revealed you *to those whom you gave me out of the world…* I have made you known *to them*' (which in both cases means the apostles) (John 17:6, 26). When His apostles watched Jesus, they saw the revelation on earth of all that it is possible for a human being to see of the invisible Father God. 'Anyone who has seen me has seen the Father,' he said to them (John 14:9). John was so moved by this that he makes it the climax of his great Prologue: 'No one has ever seen God, but God the One and Only, who is at the Father's side, has made him known' (John 1:18). Years later, in his first letter, he writes with awe of the fellowship that resulted from this revelation, 'our fellowship…with the Father and with his Son, Jesus Christ' (1 John 1:3). This is why Paul could say of Jesus Christ that, 'all the treasures of wisdom and knowledge' are found in Him, and that, 'in Christ all the fullness of the Deity lives in bodily form' (Col. 2:3, 9).

It is a wonderful thing that this unique group of apostolic eye-witnesses should be drawn into fellowship with the Father God through Jesus. And yet there is a promise here which is even more wonderful. Jesus' prayer not only looks back ('I have made you known'); it also looks forward and promises,

'I…*will continue* to make you known.' (John 17:26).

For me this is one of the most moving promises in the Bible. Jesus commits Himself to continuing to make the Father known after He has left this earth. And this ongoing revelation of the Father is the only way that the love of God continues to break into a loveless

Introduction

and lost world. Jesus says to the Father that He will continue to make Him known, 'in order that the love you have for me may be in them…' The love the Father has for Jesus is infinite and eternal. It is the love for the Son who lived for all eternity 'in the bosom of the Father' (John 1:18 KJV). That love is the source of all love. There is nothing more significant for the history of the world than for that love to overflow into men and women on earth.

In his classic book *Knowing God*, J.I. Packer writes,

> 'You sum up the whole of New Testament teaching in a single phrase, if you speak of it as the revelation of the Fatherhood of the holy Creator. In the same way, you sum up the whole of New Testament religion if you describe it as the knowledge of God as one's holy Father. If you want to judge how well a person understands Christianity, find out how much he makes of the thought of being God's child, of having God as his Father.'[6]

Packer goes on to quote from the hymn Charles Wesley wrote when he came to a lively and vital faith in Christ, 'Where shall my wondering soul begin?' in which he wrote,

> 'O how shall I the goodness tell,
> *Father*, which thou to me hast showed?
> That I, a child of wrath and hell,
> I should be called *a child of God*…'

This book explores how Jesus continues to make the Father known today. More precisely, it explores the relationship between the past, 'I have made known', and the present and future, 'I will continue to make known'. It is a wonderful and vital subject. The answer is going to focus on the work of God the Holy Spirit and the purpose and function of the Bible. In contemporary jargon, you might say this book was about the sometimes controversial topic of 'Word and Spirit'. But I have deliberately tied it to this question of making the Father known, and I have done so for two reasons.

---

6   J. I. Packer, *Knowing God* (London: Hodder and Stoughton, 1973), p. 224

First, I want to headline the Trinitarian nature of the question. Emil Brunner has said that,

> 'For every civilization, for every period of history, it is true to say: "Show me what kind of God you have, and I will tell you what kind of a humanity you possess".'[7]

Christian people believe the One true God is Father, Son and Holy Spirit. But (partly because we do so little study of early church history) many of us neglect to speak and think of God in clearly Trinitarian terms. A Bible seminary student in the United States wrote, 'I've professed the Trinity before, but now I see that I've basically worshipped and lived as a Unitarian. The church failed to explain to me what the Trinity is and why it matters.'[8] He may speak for more of us than we like to think.

One of the reasons we drift into error when thinking about the Holy Spirit is that we tend to envisage Him – as Vaughan Roberts once put it – doing a little sideshow somehow only loosely connected to the main stage where God the Father and God the Son are doing the work of salvation. Whenever we do that we are on the road to error. For the Holy Spirit is not the black sheep of the Trinity, a 'go-it-alone God' doing His own thing. God the Holy Trinity always works in harmony. As theologians sometimes express it, everything the three Persons of the Holy Trinity do outside of their own relationships within the Godhead, they do together, cooperating in perfect harmony. We cannot understand God the Holy Spirit apart from God the Son and God the Father.

My second reason for tying this study of the Spirit and the Word to 'making the Father known' is that I want to signal at the start the profound pastoral implications of getting this right. This is not some abstruse theological controversy or debate we

---

7   Emil Brunner, *Man in Revolt: A Christian Anthropology* (Cambridge, England: Lutterworth, 1939), p. 34

8   quoted in Daniel J. Trier and David Lauber (eds.), *Trinitarian Theology for the Church* (Nottingham: IVP/Apollos, 2009), p. 239

may safely leave to the experts. Whether or not we know the Father depends on these truths. Every Christian ought to strive to understand them aright.

Don't keep Spirit and Word in balance!

Before we launch into our main study, we need to guard ourselves against a common and wrong way of thinking. I recently looked up a church website and found that they described themselves as 'a word and Spirit church'. I take it that description was shorthand for something, and I got some idea what they meant by looking at the rest of the website; broadly speaking, that particular church meant that the Bible is not enough and we need the Spirit to give supplementary revelations from God. Others, for example the 'Fellowship of Word and Spirit' will mean something different.

But behind the use of the phrase can sometimes lie the idea that the ideal is somehow to have both word and Spirit in our church life, and ideally in some kind of balance. We see this in the disgruntled critic I have just quoted, suggesting there was 'too much word and not enough Spirit.' A book about the Holy Spirit had a commendation in it, which said, 'There are many who emphasise the word but neglect the Spirit. There are also many who emphasise the Spirit but neglect the word. There are few who keep both *in balance...*' (my italics). It almost feels as if a church is being watched by a kind of theological psephologist, with their Word/Spirit 'swingometer,' measuring to see if there has been a shift of a few points in one or other direction.

This must be wrong[9]. You cannot measure Bible and Spirit against one another. You cannot set Bible and Spirit side by side and say we need more of one or less of the other. It would be like saying, 'which is bigger, a metre or a litre?' Or perhaps – to use closer analogies – it would be like saying, 'That was a good

---

9   This point is also noted by John Woodhouse in 'The preacher and the living Word: preaching and the Holy Spirit' in *When God's Voice is Heard*, eds. Christopher Green and David Jackman (Leicester: IVP, 2003 edition), pp. 44-6.

concert. I just wish we had had a bit less of the violin and more of the violinist'; or to visit a workshop and say, 'it seems to me you have too much of the carpenter and not enough of the saw.' The idea of keeping them 'in balance' is a confusion of categories. The Spirit is the Sovereign God, the personal eternal Holy Spirit, the Third Person of the Trinity. No one and nothing can be measured or balanced against Him. We cannot ever reach a point where we say, 'Right, now we have enough of the Spirit. Let's have a bit more Word' or to say, 'I think we've got the balance wrong and we need a bit more Spirit.' We ought to see through the error of speaking of Word and Spirit in balance. We want to be joyfully unbalanced, setting no limits to the extent and depth of the Spirit's work for which we long. For knowing the Father depends upon Him. But let us be sure it is the Holy Spirit we seek, for He has many rivals waiting in the wings to dress up in His clothes and mimic Him.

OVERVIEW

Here is how we are going to come at the question. John's Gospel is going to be our main guide, with sideways glances at other parts of the Bible. I take it that John writes for the church as it will continue after he and the other apostles have died. And it seems that one of his great aims is to open up for us just how the Lord Jesus will continue to make the Father known. John's Gospel is perhaps the most self-consciously and explicitly Trinitarian of all the New Testament books, and I think it will be our best way in. This book is going carefully to develop a sustained argument, each part building on previous parts. It is important, therefore, patiently to follow the argument through in sequence.

In chapter 1, mainly from the first half of John's Gospel, we are going to think about Jesus the eternal Word (as John calls him in John 1:1-3) and the words He spoke. We shall see an intimate connection between the two, and see how Jesus made the Father known by words. Chapter 2 is also mainly from the first half of John's Gospel, and focuses on the weakness of Jesus' words and His paradoxical failure effectively to reveal the Father until after the Cross and therefore until the Holy Spirit was poured out on God's people. This will highlight for us how vital is the work of the Spirit. Chapter 3 explores the vital provision Jesus made for the continuation of His words through the Spirit-led teaching of His apostles. Then in chapter 4 we draw the line from the words of Jesus, through the words of His apostles, to the words of the Bible, both New Testament and Old Testament. We ask the question, 'Where do we find the words of Jesus today, since Jesus is no longer physically on earth?' It is all very well saying how wonderful were His words, but that does us no good unless we can still hear them. We shall see that every Bible word is Jesus' word, and that we cannot and must not separate Jesus the Eternal Word from Bible words. This is a vital link to establish, for – if it is true – it means we have access to Jesus' words today, and the Father can be made known to us too.

Chapter 5 is a harder chapter. You may prefer to omit this on first reading and perhaps come back to it later. It builds on the argument of chapters 3 and 4 to ask what principles ought to guide us in interpreting the Bible so we understand it aright. In chapter 6 we think about why it matters to be Bible Christians. We shall see that there are plenty of spirits out there just waiting to put on the Holy Spirit's clothes and pretend to be Him. It is an important cautionary study. Then in chapter 7 we take a good look at the wonderful work the Holy Spirit does both in the non-Christian world and in the Christian church. Finally, in conclusion, we ask how we today can listen to the Spirit, and how this relates to the Bible. In all our study, we must remember that knowing the Father depends upon these truths.

STUDY AND DISCUSSION QUESTIONS

1. Review the four common reasons why the subject of the Spirit and the Word is important. What experience do you have of any or all of them? What about the experiences of others you know?

2. Review the section about 'Making the Father known'. How important is it, in your actual Christian experience, to know God as your Father?

3. When you think and speak of God, to what extent do you consciously think of God as Father, Son and Holy Spirit?

4. Why should we avoid speaking of keeping the Spirit and the Word in balance?

1

The Spirit, the Word and His words

How did Jesus of Nazareth make the Father known during His earthly life and ministry? If making the Father known was at the heart of His reason for coming to earth, it is important to know the answer, which may surprise us.

It was not by His physical appearance, for all the evidence suggests that He looked just like lots of other men of His race and culture. His cousin John the Baptist had to point him out ('Look!'), otherwise no one would have noticed Him when He mingled with the crowds at John's preaching and baptisms (John 1:29-36). We like to imagine Him with a distinctive beard, different clothing, implausible blue eyes, and the film director's halo to mark Him out as special. But Isaiah's prophecy was true, 'He had no beauty or majesty to attract us to him, nothing in his appearance that we should desire (that is, admire and be attracted to) him' (Isa. 53:2). He looked quite normal. We would not have been able to pick out Jesus from a still photo of a crowd of which He was part; only a video would have revealed Him, when we saw and heard how He spoke and related with people[1].

---

[1] I am grateful to my colleague and friend Robin Weekes for this analogy.

Nor was it His miracles that made the Father known – or at least not the miracles on their own. For a miracle-worker could go around doing all sorts of extraordinary things; but unless those miracles were explained and interpreted, they would mean nothing. He might be nothing more than an extraordinary circus freak of nature, for all that anyone would know better. John characteristically speaks of Jesus' miracles as 'signs,' because they were signposts pointing to His identity and work. And they were only signposts because of the words that accompanied them. The healing of the man by the pool meant nothing without the teaching of the rest of John 5. The feeding of the 5,000 was ambiguous without the discourse of John 6. Sight to a man born blind meant little without the 'light of the world' teaching of John 9 and 10. Even the raising of Lazarus had to be interpreted by words in John 11. Even His death on the Cross only revealed the Father because it was interpreted by words. Many men were crucified by the Romans. It is only the words that surround this crucifixion that enable us to understand what it reveals and achieves.

It was neither by His physical appearance nor even by His miracles that Jesus made the Father known. It was by His words. We are going to consider the wonder, the origin, the nature and the enduring significance of Jesus' words.

THE WONDER OF JESUS' WORDS

When the temple security forces returned to their seniors empty-handed, having failed to arrest Jesus, they pleaded with amazement that, 'No-one ever spoke the way this man does' (John 7:46). Never in the history of the world had a man spoken as Jesus spoke. Luke tells us something very similar. When Jesus taught in his home synagogue in Nazareth, they 'were amazed at the gracious words that came from his lips' (Luke 4:22).

It must have been an extraordinary experience to hear Jesus of Nazareth teach. We must try to imagine the most beautiful, wise and gracious teaching we have ever heard, and then – in our minds – to purge it of all selfishness, all malice, all foolishness, all poor judgement, all ugliness, all incompleteness, anything inappropriate, all inadequacy, all superficiality, all half-truths and any trace of misleading exaggeration or untruth. We cannot think of such perfect speech, even in our most optimistic imagination. And yet this is what it must have been, to hear Jesus speak, whether it was a public set-piece teaching or a private 'off-the-cuff' conversation with an individual. When tired as when fresh, when pressured as when relaxed, when opposed as when applauded, no-one ever spoke as this man.

Jesus' words were wonderful and beautiful words. And by those words He made the Father known. In the prayer of John 17 (which we quoted in the Introduction), Jesus says to the Father,

> 'I have revealed you to those whom you gave me out of the world… For *I gave them the words you gave me* and they accepted them.' (John 17:6, 8).

He gave them words, the words the Father had first given Him, and by those words He revealed the Father.

John especially draws attention to the words that Jesus spoke and His role as a teacher. Words like 'Rabbi', 'Teacher', 'word', 'words', 'teaching', 'testimony' and 'testify' abound. The first disciples called Him, '"Rabbi" (which means Teacher)' (John 1:38). When Nicodemus comes to Him by night he too begins, 'Rabbi, we know you are a teacher come from God…' (John 3:2). Jesus says that it is those who hear His word and believe the Father who sent Him, who have eternal life (John 5:24). At the end of the long discourse of chapter 6, John says, 'He said this while teaching in the synagogue in Capernaum' (John 6:59). Teaching is what Jesus characteristically did. He testifies against the world (John 7:7). He says, 'If anyone chooses to do God's will, he will find out whether my teaching comes from God or whether I speak on my own' (John 7:17).

In the controversy of John 8, Jesus claims, 'If you hold to my teaching, you are really my disciples' (John 8:31). He says to His enemies, 'you are ready to kill me, because you have no room for my word' (John 8:37). If anyone keeps Jesus' 'word' he will never see death (John 8:51). At His trial the high priest questions Jesus 'about his disciples and his teaching' (John 18:19). He tells Pontius Pilate that, 'for this reason I was born, and for this I came into the world, to testify to the truth' (John 18:37).

When John recounts the wonder of the apostolic testimony at the start of his first letter, he begins, 'That which was from the beginning, which we have heard...' (1 John 1:1). He goes on to the fact that they saw, looked upon and touched. But he begins with what they heard. So there is this massive emphasis on the wonder of Jesus' words.

THE ORIGIN OF JESUS' WORDS

But how did it come to be that His words were so perfect, so wise and so gracious? John points us to the origin of Jesus' words for an answer. He does it in two complementary ways.

1 ...in the eternal life of the Father

First, he directs us to their origin with the Father Himself. At the very start of his Gospel, he bookends his great Prologue in this way,

> 'In the beginning was the Word, and the Word was with God and the Word was God. He was with God in the beginning...' (John 1:1, 2)

> '...No-one has ever seen God, but God the One and Only, who is at the Father's side' (literally, 'in the Father's bosom', in the closest possible intimacy with the Father), 'has made him known.' (John 1:18).

The Word is personal ('he'), He has an identity distinct from God the Father (He is 'with God,' 'at the Father's side'), and yet He is Himself 'God'. He is the Word who makes the Father known.

The root idea of a word is self-expression. Our words are both part of us (for they originate in our hearts) and yet distinct

The Spirit, the Word and His words

from us (for they go out from our mouths). The question arises in human affairs whether or not we will be true to the word we have spoken. For God, there is no such question: the Father was, is, and will always be, true to the eternal Word He spoke in Jesus. And Jesus perfectly expresses the heart and name of the Father who spoke Him. He is the perfect eternal self-expression of the Father.

2 ...given by the anointing of the Spirit

The other way in which John teaches us to understand the origin of Jesus' words is by pointing to His anointing with the Spirit after His baptism by John the Baptist. Jesus is both the eternal pre-existent divine Word and – at the same time – the fully human man upon whom the Spirit of God descends and remains. John the Baptist gives this testimony about Jesus' baptism,

> 'I saw the Spirit come down from heaven as a dove and remain on him. I would not have known him, except that the one who sent me to baptise with water told me, "The man on whom you see the Spirit come down and remain is he who will baptise with the Holy Spirit." I have seen and I testify that this is the Son of God.' (John 1:32-34).

Twice John includes the words, 'and remain', emphasising that the anointing of Jesus with the Spirit was permanent. Although John the Baptist was Jesus' relative (Luke 1:36), and no doubt knew who Jesus was (in a superficial sense), he testifies that it was only when he paradoxically 'saw' the invisible Spirit of God come down and remain on Jesus that he 'knew' in a deep sense who Jesus was and Jesus could be 'revealed to Israel' (John 1:31).

Jesus Christ – Son of the Father and man anointed by the Spirit

John sets side by side two ways of thinking about Jesus Christ[2]. First, he gives us what is sometimes called a Word-Christology.

---

2   for a more technical discussion of this section, see Telford Work, *Living and Active: Scripture in the Economy of Salvation* (Grand Rapids, Michigan: Eerdmans,

Christology means learning to think and talk about Christ. A Word-Christology means thinking of Him as the 'Word' of John 1:1, 2, pre-existent, the one who had been God the Son in intimate proximity with the Father from all eternity.

Alongside this he gives us what is sometimes called a Spirit-Christology. This means thinking of Jesus Christ as the fully human man anointed with the Spirit of God. The word translated 'anointed' is the same word from which we get 'Christ'. A Christ (the Greek word) or Messiah (the Hebrew word) means an anointed one. In his Nazareth synagogue sermon Jesus spoke of Isaiah's prophetic anointing being fulfilled in His messianic anointing: 'The Spirit of the Lord is on me, because he has anointed' – we might say 'Christed' – 'me…' (Luke 4:18 quoting from Isa. 61:1). And in Acts 10 Peter describes 'how God anointed' – again, we might say, 'Christed' – 'Jesus of Nazareth with the Holy Spirit and (therefore) with power' (Acts 10:38).

Both ways of thinking are true and we need them both. Remembering that Jesus is the Eternal Word safeguards us from the mistake of thinking that Jesus only became the Son of God, at His baptism, when the Spirit came upon Him. This error is called 'adoptionism' as if God looked around for a man to adopt as His Son, and happened to fix upon Jesus of Nazareth.

Considering that Jesus is the man of the Spirit reminds us that He was (and is) fully human. Indeed, it does seem that there was a change in Jesus' experience at the time of His baptism. From the time of His conception, Jesus was 'God with us' (Immanuel, Matt.1:23). But from the time of His baptism, the Spirit was – if we may say this reverently – 'God with Jesus' to equip Him with power for ministry. This is why there were no miracles before Jesus was anointed with the Spirit. He who had

2002), pp. 118-20.

always been the Son of God in His nature entered only then on His public ministry of revealing the Father.

From His conception to His baptism, Jesus' life was surrounded, as it were, by the special ministry of the Spirit[3]. Even in Jesus' childhood, when Mary and Joseph found him in the temple, 'Everyone who heard him was amazed at his understanding and his answers' (Luke 2:47). But John ascribes the revelatory power of Jesus' words especially to the abiding presence with Him of the Spirit after His baptism. At the end of John 3 there is a little explanatory comment about Jesus (John 3:31-36)[4]. In it we read that,

> 'the one whom God has sent speaks the words of God, for God gives the Spirit without limit.' (John 3:34)

John says that, 'the one whom God has sent' (that is, Jesus) 'speaks the words of God'; and the reason He does so is because 'God' (that is, God the Father) 'gives the Spirit' (that is, to God the Son) 'without limit'. The reason Jesus Christ speaks the exact words of God the Father is that God the Father has given to Him the Spirit of God without any limit. This is unique. When the New Testament later speaks of the Spirit being given to Christian believers, it never speaks of Him being given to an individual believer in an unlimited way. Rather, His gifts and working are apportioned out to us in partial ways (e.g. 1 Cor. 12:7-11). But to Jesus, He was given without limit. And therefore His words perfectly revealed the Father.

We must notice the Trinitarian nature of all this. The eternal Son speaks the words of the eternal Father by the ministry of the eternal Spirit. He has heard and known those words from all eternity, dwelling in the bosom of the Father in unbroken and unimaginable intimacy. And now in His human incarnation

---

3   Luke especially emphasizes this in his telling of the gospel.

4   In some English translations this section is printed as a continuing part of the direct speech of John the Baptist, following on from verses 27-30. This is possible, but it seems more likely this is John the gospel-writer's comment (see Köstenberger for a concise summary of reasons).

He knows those words again, perfectly and completely, by the ministry of God the Holy Spirit coming upon Him and abiding with him without any boundary to limit the completeness of His filling and intimacy.

This is why no-one ever spoke as Jesus spoke. This is why He tells Nicodemus that He speaks about what He knows and gives testimony to what He has seen (John 3:11). This is why He can say of His teaching that it 'is not my own. It comes from him who sent me' (John 7:16). This is why he could say, 'I…speak just what the Father has taught me… I am telling you what I have seen in the Father's presence' (John 8:28, 38). This union with God the Father and God the Holy Spirit is the source and origin of Jesus' wonderful words.

Spirit and breath

This is a good point to pause and make the important observation that both the Hebrew and the Greek words for 'spirit' (*ruach* and *pneuma*) also mean 'breath' or 'wind'. So when a Hebrew or Greek speaker hears the word for 'spirit' they naturally think also of 'breath'. And it is a short journey from a person's 'breath' to the person's words, for words are carried on breath. A person breathes out words. So it should be no surprise to us that the man of the Spirit of God is the man of the words of God. Indeed, it would be strange if he were not. We shall note this connection again.[5]

THE NATURE OF JESUS' WORDS

We now shift our focus from the divine origin of Jesus' words (the words of God the Father spoken by God the Son through the ministry of God the Holy Spirit) to the spiritual and life-giving nature of Jesus' words. The one follows from the other.

We find the most striking testimony to the nature of Jesus' words in two sayings near the end of John chapter 6,

---

5   I am grateful to John Woodhouse for this observation, which he has developed in 'The preacher and the living Word', chapter 3 of *When God's Voice is Heard* (Leicester: IVP, 2003), pp. 55-9.

The Spirit, the Word and His words

'The words I have spoken to you are spirit and they are life'
(Jesus in John 6:63)

'You have the words of eternal life' (Peter in John 6:68)

John 6 begins (vv. 1-13) with the feeding of the 5,000. That
wonderful feeding is the springboard for the teaching that
follows, which is all about food. After the feeding, the people
try to make Jesus king by force (v. 15). But He withdraws. That
evening He walks on the water to join His disciples in the boat
crossing to the other side of the Sea of Galilee (vv. 16-23).
The crowds that had been at the feeding cross over in other
boats and find Him in Capernaum, on the west side of the lake
(vv. 24, 25). Jesus' extended teaching about food runs, with brief
interruptions, from verse 26 through to verse 59. He contrasts
physical food (the bread of the miraculous feeding) with 'food
that endures to eternal life' (v. 27), that is, food that will feed
you spiritually and keep you alive for the age to come. When
they ask what they must 'do' Jesus says they must 'believe' in
Him (vv. 28, 29). Using the image of the manna-bread given
by God to the Israelites in the wilderness after the Exodus
(Exod. 16), Jesus describes Himself as the reality to which this
foreshadowing pointed ('I am the Bread of life' v. 35). He tells
them that to get the life of the age to come they need to eat
Him, and go on eating Him. Indeed, the 'bread' they must eat
is His 'flesh' which He will give for the life of the world (v.
51). It sounds horrifying. So, again, the question comes, how
can it be possible to do that (v. 52)? Jesus replies they must
eat His 'flesh' and drink His 'blood', where flesh and blood in
separation speak of a life given up in death. So in some spiritual
way they must feed on the death of Jesus.

Clearly He is speaking of a spiritual feeding. But what does
it mean? There are several reasons for concluding that Jesus is
not telling people to eat and drink the bread and wine of Holy
Communion or the Lord's Supper. That would have made
no sense to His original hearers, since the Last Supper hadn't
happened and the Lord's Supper hadn't been instituted. None

of the very earliest commentators thought He meant that. Again and again He tells us that it's about believing in Him (vv. 35, 40, 47), which is an inward and spiritual thing. It is true that the Lord's Supper or Holy Communion is the outward and physical sign that points to this inward reality. But we do not feed on Jesus by the mere outward action of taking communion. We feed on Him in our hearts by faith (as Cranmer put it in the Book of Common Prayer). 'John 6 is not about the Lord's Supper; rather, the Lord's Supper is about what is described in John 6.'[6]

The section that immediately follows (vv. 60-9) gives us the clue as to what Jesus means. In verses 60 and 66 many of Jesus' followers are so horrified by this strange teaching that they turn back. Jesus expands on His teaching in verse 63: 'The Spirit gives life; the flesh counts for nothing.' That is to say, only the Spirit of God can give the life of God. We shall think more about this in chapter 2. He went on to say, 'The words I have spoken to you are spirit and they are life.' That is to say, the wonderful divine words spoken by Jesus are in the deepest possible sense spiritual (or Holy Spirit) words; they are the 'breath/spirit' of God; and therefore these words – and these words alone – will give a man or woman spiritual life, the life of the age to come. So eating Jesus, in the vivid imagery of this chapter, means taking the words of Jesus, believing them, taking them inside ourselves and internalising them[7]. Of course, Jesus' words are not the same as Jesus Himself. It is Jesus Himself who gives spiritual life. It is Jesus who draws us into the life of the living Trinity. It is 'Christ in you' who is our hope of glory and Christ who is our life (Col. 1:27; 3:4). But that life is mediated to us by His spiritual life-giving words.

When we 'eat' Jesus' words, we will at the same time appropriate by faith for ourselves all the benefits of His death.

---

6   Colin Brown quoted in D. A. Carson, *The Gospel according to John* (Leicester: IVP, 1991), p. 280

7   We have a lovely Old Testament example of this internalising, in Jeremiah 15:16 'When your words came, I ate them; they were my joy and my heart's delight.'

The Spirit, the Word and His words

The Lord's Supper is indeed a vivid dramatisation and visible sign of that inward and spiritual feeding. But it is not the feeding itself. That is a matter of the heart, and it comes through words. So it is by words that we are nourished, given life and kept alive for the age to come, by the Father's words spoken by Jesus. These words can change us. They can get inside us and change our thinking, our hearts, our wills and our emotions. These words shape us. They move us. It is by Jesus' words that we feed upon Jesus in our hearts by faith, by hearing His words, listening, heeding, paying close attention, mulling them over, obeying them and sharing them. For these words are precisely, word for word, the words given by the Father to Jesus. These words make the Father known.

So it is quite a theme: Jesus reveals the Father by speaking the words the Father had given Him. In his excellent book *Words of Life: Scripture as the living and active word of God,* Timothy Ward rightly suggests that the Father gave Jesus these words in eternity, that is that these words open to us something of 'the communicative activity that exists between the persons of the Trinity'. In which case, as Ward points out, it is not surprising that they are quite literally 'full of the Spirit', the breath of God Himself. 'For how could words that have their origin in God and that God names as his own be anything else?'[8]. These words of Jesus are the overflow on earth of the life and love of the Holy Trinity in eternity.

THE ENDURING SIGNIFICANCE OF JESUS' WORDS

Finally, I want us to see how Jesus Himself indicated, during His earthly ministry, that in some way it was particularly His words that would have enduring significance. Clearly His physical appearance could have no enduring significance, since He would no longer be visible on earth. And, as we have seen, it never was significant anyway. But nor could His mighty deeds be of enduring significance on their own, since men and women after His Ascension could not see the deeds He had done, and He would no longer be physically present on earth to continue doing

---

8   Timothy Ward, *Words of Life* (Nottingham: IVP, 2009), p. 40f

them. (We shall consider in chapter 3 the significance of the miracles done by the agency of others after Jesus' Ascension.)

I want to focus on a very important, and somewhat neglected, summary passage in John 12. Chapter 12 is a kind of hinge chapter in John's Gospel. It lies between what is sometimes called 'the book of signs' (ch. 1–11) and the sufferings that are the focus of chapters 13–19. At the end of verse 36, we read,

> 'When he had finished speaking, Jesus left and hid himself from them.'

This marks the end of His public ministry. He will not appear in public again except during His trial and on the Cross.

Verses 37-43 are John's summing-up of the results of Jesus' public ministry. And then in verses 44-50 he gives us one more public declaration of Jesus:

> 'And Jesus cried out and said…'

While it is possible that this records teaching that Jesus gave on a later occasion when He came out of hiding, it seems more likely that this is John's summary of all of Jesus' public teaching before He went into hiding. This speech has the feel of 'an epilogue rather than a speech within the main structure of the play.'[9] It concludes chapters 1–12 rather as the great Prologue of John 1:1-18 opened it. If so, we may expect these seven verses to be of great significance. They are.

There is a striking and simple structure to them. In verses 44-46 Jesus speaks about Himself; seven times He says 'me' or 'I'. And then in verses 47-50 He speaks almost exclusively about His words. Verses 44-46 sum up the great theme of the gospel so far,

> 'When a man believes in *me*, he does not believe in *me* only, but in the one who sent *me*. When he looks at *me*, he sees the one who sent *me*. *I* have come into the world as a light, so that no-one who believes in *me* should stay in darkness.'

---

9   C. K. Barrett, *The Gospel according to St. John* (2nd Edition. London: SPCK, 1978), p. 429

The Spirit, the Word and His words

To believe in Jesus is to believe in the Father. To look (with faith) at Jesus is to look at the Father. To believe and look with faith at Jesus is therefore to come out of the darkness of this world into the light that comes from the Father. Jesus makes the Father known.

But then in verses 47-50 the focus shifts from Jesus Himself to His words. Although He continues to speak of Himself ('I', 'me', 'my') He now wants us to learn something about His words,

> 'As for the person who hears *my words* but does not keep them, I do not judge him. For I did not come to judge the world, but to save it. There is a judge for the one who rejects me and does not accept *my words*; *that very word which I spoke* will condemn him at the last day. For I did not *speak* of my own accord, but the Father who sent me commanded me *what to say* and how to say it [literally, 'what to say and what to speak']. I know that his command leads to eternal life. So *whatever I say* is just *what the Father has told me to say.*'

To 'keep' Jesus' words means both to do them and also to preserve them, passing them on to the next generation[10]. To hear Jesus' words and not keep them will mean we are judged in the end precisely by 'that very word' which Jesus spoke. To reject Jesus is the same as not accepting (or receiving) His words ('the one who rejects me and does not accept my words…'). The reason for the enduring significance of His words is that these words are precisely the words given Him by the Father.

This points to the future, after Jesus' death, resurrection and Ascension. When the physical Jesus is no longer on earth, when He is no longer here for witnesses to watch Him perform miracles, His words will endure. From now on He will not be known 'from a worldly point of view' (2 Cor. 5:16), not by His appearance, but by His voice. His sheep will hear His voice (John 10:3). The dead will hear His voice (John 5:25, 28) as Lazarus had done (John 11:43). Mary Magdalene will recognise Him, not by seeing Him, but by hearing His voice call her name (John 20:14, 16).

---

10   Peter Adam, *Written for Us* (Nottingham: IVP, 2008), p. 232

From now on until He returns, it is our response to the words and voice of Jesus that determines our destiny.

CONCLUSION

Jesus made the Father known by words. They were wonderful words, words whose origins lay in the intimate fellowship of the Father and the Son in eternity, words given to Jesus in His incarnate state by the ministry of the Holy Spirit, words whose nature was in the deepest sense spirit and life. They were Holy Spirit words, God words, words that men and women need to 'eat' to have the life of the age to come. After Jesus leaves, our response to these words is response to Him. Rejection of these words is rejection of Him.

So the really important question is, where do we find His words and how can we hear His voice today? We shall wait until chapters 3 and 4 before we answer that question.

STUDY AND DISCUSSION QUESTIONS

1. How do we know that Jesus did not reveal the Father by His physical appearance? And by His miracles on their own?

2. Trace the significance of Jesus' words and teaching through John chapters 1–11. How does John draw attention to the importance of this? (For example, look at John 3:2; 5:24; 7:46; 8:31, 37, 51)

3. Look in particular for the way John and Jesus Himself point us to the divine origin of Jesus' words both as coming from the Father and as given by the ministry of the Spirit? (For example, look at John 3:34; 6:63, 68; 7:16, 17; 8:28, 38)

4. Try to explain in your own words what it meant for Jesus to be at the same time the eternal Son and Word of the Father, and also the man uniquely anointed by the Spirit? In particular, how do you think we can understand the change in Jesus' experience from the time of His baptism?

5. Read John 12:44-50. How does Jesus speak of the ongoing significance of His words? Why do you think John puts this summary speech at this point of his telling of the story?

2

The Spirit, the Word
and the Cross

In chapter 1 we considered the wonder, the origin, the nature and the enduring significance of Jesus' words. In chapters 3 and 4 we will ask where those words are to be found so that we may hear them today. But in this chapter we have to face a terrible and sobering fact: Jesus failed. We will see in this chapter the weakness of Jesus' words until the Spirit was poured out.

THE FAILURE OF JESUS' EARTHLY MINISTRY
The earthly ministry of Jesus was an almost complete failure, as it was always bound to be, as God knew it must be, and as Jesus said it would be. At the end of His public teaching ministry, Jesus hides Himself and never teaches in public again (John 12:36). And immediately, John sums it up like this:

> 'Even after Jesus had done all these miraculous signs in their presence, they still would not believe in him' (John 12:37).

For three years the eternal Word of God spoke the living words of God. He backed up those words by living the flawless life of God and by working the awesome works of God. His words were powerfully supported by His deeds, and never for one moment undermined by inconsistency or hypocrisy in His life. And yet almost no-one heard Him. The Word became flesh and almost nobody recognised that they were seeing His glory. And those few who did have some idea, didn't realise quite what they were seeing until much later. He revealed the Father and nobody noticed. They noticed *Him*, for He worked miracles; but they didn't see the Father. Many hated Him or were indifferent. A few followed for a while but most fell away (John 6:66). He hand-picked twelve and one of them turned out to be 'a devil' (John 6:70). The others deserted Him at the end. None of them understood His words. For three years He made the Father known, and at the end of that time one of His inner circle spoke for them all when he asked Him, 'Show us the Father' (John 14:8). It was an extraordinary failure.

We need to explore why Jesus failed, for it has a deep impact on our subject of Jesus making the Father known today. Only after He left this world did people believe and understand. Suddenly, in their thousands and then millions, a multitude that no man can number, they believed. So what had changed? Before we find hope, our search will inject much-needed sober realism into our subject, for it speaks to us of our helplessness, our deep darkness and our utter inability to find the Father God for ourselves.

The elusiveness of Jesus

First, let us observe a general theme in John's portrayal of Jesus: Jesus is elusive[1]. In his Prologue, John says that, 'The light shines in the darkness, but the darkness has not understood it' (John 1:5). The word translated 'understood' means something like 'grasped' and includes both grasping with the hands (that is, arresting someone, or making them captive) and grasping with the mind (understanding someone). Jesus can neither be apprehended nor comprehended. The world can neither control Him nor understand Him. Although He is fully human,

---

1   See Mark Stibbe, *John's Gospel* (London: Routledge, 1994), pp. 5-31

The Spirit, the Word and the Cross

He is a deeply elusive figure. The world does not 'recognise' Him (John 1:10). Later in chapter 1, John the Baptist says to the people that, 'among you stands one *you do not know*' who needs to 'be *revealed* to Israel' for unless He is revealed they will not know who He is (John 1:26, 31).

Jesus tells puzzling riddles, such as, 'Destroy this temple, and I will raise it again in three days' (John 2:19). They do not understand Him at the time. He uses strange language, such as new birth, which Nicodemus does not understand (John 3:1-10). He speaks of living water, which the Samaritan woman cannot grasp (John 4:10-15). In John 5 Jesus does a wonderful healing of a man paralysed for thirty-eight years, and then, when they ask the healed man who had healed him, John comments, 'The man who was healed had no idea who it was (that healed him), for Jesus had slipped away into the crowd that was there' (John 5:13). He is there when He chooses to be there, and not at our summoning. Something similar happens in chapter 9 when He heals a man born blind. He sends the man off to wash in the Pool of Siloam (John 9:7), and by the time he returns Jesus has slipped away, and does not appear again on the scene until verse 35. Although this man knows Jesus' name (v. 11), he does not see Him until verses 35-38. He saw Jesus only when Jesus 'found him' (v. 35).

After the feeding of the 5,000, when they want to make Jesus king, He 'withdrew… to a mountain by himself' for He will not be governed by anyone else's agenda (John 6:15). That night, when His disciples are making heavy weather of rowing across the lake, Jesus suddenly appears out of nowhere, walking on the water, unexpectedly (John 6:19). In chapter 7 He tells His brothers He is not going up with them to the Feast of Tabernacles, but then later slips into Jerusalem secretly, for He comes and goes as He chooses and will not be cajoled or summoned by anyone (John 7:10).

Three times people try to arrest Him and fail:

> '…they tried to seize him, but no-one laid a hand on him, because his time had not yet come.' (John 7:30)

'Some wanted to seize him, but no-one laid a hand on him.'
(John 7:44)

'Again they tried to seize him, but he escaped their grasp.'
(John 10:39)

Twice He hides Himself:

'...they picked up stones to stone him, but Jesus hid himself,
slipping away from the temple grounds.' (John 8:59)

'When he had finished speaking, Jesus left and hid himself
from them.' (John 12:36)

He says He is going somewhere they cannot follow:

'You will look for me, but you will not find me; and where
I am, you cannot come.' (John 7:34)

He is only arrested when He deliberately goes to the garden where
He knows Judas will come to find Him. And even when the
arrest party arrive in the garden, it is only when Jesus 'went out'
to them and identifies Himself, that they manage to arrest Him
(John 18:1-8). Even when arrested, it is clear that Jesus is in control.

Consistently, Jesus is in control. He appears when and where
He chooses, and He hides Himself whenever He chooses. You
cannot find Jesus; He finds you. You cannot identify Jesus; He
reveals Himself. You cannot understand Jesus; He explains
Himself. This is deeply humbling. At the conclusion of the
healing of the man born blind, we read:

'Jesus said, "For judgement I have come into this world, so
that the blind will see and those who see will become blind."
Some Pharisees who were with him heard him say this and
asked, "What? Are we blind too?" Jesus said, "If you were
blind, you would not be guilty of sin; but now that you claim
you can see, your guilt remains."' (John 9:39-41)

William Temple comments, 'It is a crushing, overwhelming
retort. Can we escape its impact? Only in one of two ways. Either
we must confess our blindness and seek the opening of our eyes;

or else we must accept the light and walk by it. What we may not do, yet all strive to do, is to keep our eyes half-open and live by half the light. That kind of sight holds us to our sin and our sin to us. But the only way of avoiding it is to look with eyes wide open upon ourselves and the world as the full light reveals it; but this is the surrender of faith, and pride resists it.'[2]

Claiming to see is the big mistake the Pharisees made. If I think I am in control, that I can see, then I will utterly miss Jesus Christ. Only those who confess their blindness, acknowledge their darkness, and cry out for sight have any hope. The sad general picture in John 1–12 is that men and women think they 'see' and are therefore deeply blind to Jesus and therefore do not see the Father.

THERE IS NO EVOLUTION FROM FLESH TO SPIRIT

In John chapter 3, Nicodemus comes to Jesus by night as a man of the night. He has seen signs (v. 2) but not really seen where the signposts are pointing. He cannot begin to see the Kingdom of God unless and until the Holy Spirit gives him a new birth from above (v. 3). He cannot be reasoned into the Kingdom. As the great fourth-century preacher John Chrysostom put it, 'earthly reasonings are full of mud'[3]. They are like building a Babel tower and end in confusion of tongues. He cannot be manipulated into the Kingdom. His mind 'is moving in a flatland world'[4].

He cannot even be cajoled into the Kingdom or get himself into the Kingdom. The story is told of a preacher who was always saying, 'You must be born again'. And someone asked him, 'Why do you always say you must be born again?' – to which he replied, 'Because you must be born again.' Well, it's true; you must. But it's a birth from above, not a birth we can engineer or plan for ourselves.

2   William Temple, *Readings in St. John's Gospel* (London: Macmillan, 1961), p.155f

3   John Chrysostom, *Homilies on the Gospel of St. John* (Peabody, Massachusetts: Zondervan, 'Nicene and Post-Nicene Fathers' Vol.14, 2004) ad loc.

4   Lesslie Newbigin, *The Light has Come* (Grand Rapids, Michigan: Eerdmans, 1982), p. 38

John Chrysostom puts it vividly when he wrote, 'The earthly birth which is according to the flesh, is of the dust, and therefore *heaven is walled against it*, for what hath earth in common with heaven?'[5] What is born of the flesh is flesh and will always be flesh. As another writer put is, 'There is no evolution from flesh to Spirit'[6].

At the end of John 3 there is a little section of explanatory comment (vv. 31-36), in which John paints this divide clearly:

> 'The one who comes from above is above all; the one who is from the earth belongs to the earth, and speaks as one from the earth. The one who comes from heaven is above all. He testifies to what he has seen and heard, but no-one accepts his testimony.' (John 3:31, 32)

There is this absolute divide between 'the one who comes from above' and 'the one who is from the earth' (that is, the whole human race by nature, earthly by origin). A human being by nature 'speaks as one from the earth'. Earthly identity leads to earthly speech; heavenly identity leads to heavenly speech, and until the Holy Spirit bridges the gap, never the twain shall meet. This is why 'the one who comes from heaven' testifies to what He has seen and heard in heaven, but people don't believe Him. Ever since the first human disobedience, heaven (the Bible's way of speaking about God's place) is inaccessible to earth (this space-time universe that we know).

This inaccessibility is very evident in contemporary debates with the so-called 'New Atheists,' such as Richard Dawkins, Philip Pullman and Christopher Hitchens. In his tirade against all religion, *God is not great: how religion poisons everything*, Hitchens concludes with his own proposal for 'a New Enlightenment'. He quotes with approval the eighteenth-century German sceptic Gotthold Lessing, who said that if God held out to him in his

---

5   John Chrysostom, *Homilies on the Gospel of St. John* (Peabody, Massachusetts: Zondervan, 'Nicene and Post-Nicene Fathers' Vol.14, 2004) ad loc., my italics

6   E. Hoskyns, quoted in Leon Morris, *The Gospel according to John* (Revised Edition) (Grand Rapids, Michigan: Eerdmans New International Commentary on the New Testament, 1995), p. 194

right hand 'all Truth' and in His left hand 'the steady and diligent drive for Truth, albeit with the proviso that I would always and forever err in the process'[7] and offered him the choice, he would choose the left hand. That is to say, the humble search for truth is better than the arrogant claim to have attained or found truth. So, according to this approach, the best we can hope for is a perpetual and flawed search. It is a bit like the story of Sisyphus in Homer's *Odyssey*, where Sisyphus is condemned by the gods to roll a large boulder up a hill, and it keeps rolling down again.

So, says Hitchens, what we need is 'a renewed Enlightenment, which will base itself on the proposition that the proper study of mankind is man, and woman'[8] and nothing beyond. Anthropology, not Theology, ought to be the Queen of the Sciences. But this, like Nicodemus, is life in 'a flatland world'. This is the tadpole mocking all suggestions that there might be life outside the pond. This is darkness. And until God reaches down, it will remain darkness. Heaven is walled against this world. Nothing we can do can raise 'flesh' to 'Spirit'. Sitting meditating in silence will not raise earthly thought to heavenly understanding. Music cannot metamorphose flesh into spirit. No human activity whatsoever can make flesh give birth to spirit. This is why Jesus' earthly ministry failed. It did not surprise Jesus.

THE BONDAGE OF THE WILL

John 8 is a chapter of fierce and intense controversy between Jesus and His opponents. In verses 42-47 Jesus says two hard-hitting things that help us understand our darkness:

> 'Why is my language not clear to you? Because *you are unable* to hear what I say.' (v. 43)

> 'He who belongs to God hears what God says. The reason you do not hear is that you do not belong to God.' (v. 47)

Jesus says the problem is not that He Himself is being unclear, for He is being crystal clear in these debates. The problem is

---

7   Christopher Hitchens, *God is not great* (London: Atlantic Books, 2007), p. 277

8   Ibid., p. 283

that in a deep sense they are 'unable' to hear Him because until and unless a man or woman 'belongs to God' they will not and cannot hear what God says. It is not just that they do not like what Jesus says. It is that their wills are bound by sin. This is what Martin Luther called 'The Bondage of the Will'[9] in his famous Reformation debate with Erasmus. As Luther argued, we are free to choose, but the only choice we can make by ourselves is the choice for self and against faith in God.

So Jesus' opponents hear what Jesus says, the words impact their ears. But as worldly creatures they are colour-blind to His colours, tone-deaf to His music. They *cannot* hear His 'word'. The problem is one of the will not of the intellect. At the deepest level they are alienated from what Jesus stands for, and so it is not surprising they are puzzled again and again by what He says. The missionary bishop Lesslie Newbigin writes,

'The life of man centered in the development of his own self, in the unfolding of his own capacities, is the microcosm which is reflected on the grand scale (as the word implies) in the cosmos, the organized world of human culture in all its forms – philosophy, science, technics, economics, politics, and aesthetics. "The world" represents on the grand scale man's attempt to understand and to organize his life in such a way that he is in control of it. Language, which is fundamental to the whole effort, provides the "words" by which the business of understanding and managing is carried on. The words of Jesus – his audible speech in one of the languages of the world – are part of the world. His hearers hear them. But they can only hear them as part of this world. In that context they are intolerable and must be silenced. The Jews are unable – literally unable – to hear his *logos*, the word which he himself is. And this is because the *logos* is in fact the true source and center of all that exists and its presence requires the abandonment of the whole enterprise of understanding and managing the world from

9   Martin Luther, *The Bondage of the Will* (translated J. I. Packer and O. R. Johnston. London: James Clarke, 1957)

a center in the human ego. From this center belief is simply an impossibility. It is not that the man in the world has the free option to believe or not to believe.'[10]

Newbigin goes on to say that,

'Man does not stand at a midpoint between the two, free to choose one or the other. He is part of "the world" which seeks to possess in itself light and life – the capacity to understand and the power to cope.'[11]

What Jesus says here comes as 'a shocking assault upon the sovereignty of the autonomous reason and conscience'. These opponents could see the Bible, but they could not and would not see the Christ of the Bible.

GOD BLINDS PROUD EYES

This is why, when John sums up the failure of Jesus' earthly ministry, he quotes twice from Isaiah. The second quotation, from Isaiah 6, is quoted by Jesus Himself when teaching in parables (Matt. 13:14, 15) and by Paul speaking to the unbelieving Jews in Rome (Acts 28:26, 27):

'He (God) has blinded their eyes and deadened their hearts, so that they can neither see with their eyes, nor understand with their hearts, nor turn – and I would heal them' (John 12:40)

God Himself, in just judgement upon human pride, dooms the humanist project to failure. We are by nature utterly blind and hard-hearted to the things of God. We cannot think clearly and accurately about God, and no human technique can enable us to do so. We must not begin to claim that 'we see' by our own autonomous thinking and initiative. Only when God reveals Himself to us, and the Father is made known to us from above, will we begin to get it.

---

10   Lesslie Newbigin, *The Light has Come* (Grand Rapids, Michigan: Eerdmans, 1982), p. 112

11   Ibid., p. 113

Hearing the Spirit

We desperately need the Spirit of God to take the words of God (the words spoken by Jesus the Eternal Word, the words we considered in chapter 1) and write them on our hearts. So long as these words remain outside us, they will do no more than ring in our ears. They will still be the voice of the man from heaven, but to earthly ears they will make no sense. Nicodemus needs a new birth from above by the Spirit. The Samaritan woman is told that,

> 'God is spirit, and his worshippers must worship in spirit and in truth.' (John 4:24).

This does not mean that anyone can worship God anywhere, so long as they are genuine and sincere. On the contrary, it means that only those who receive the Holy Spirit can worship Him at all! To worship God 'in spirit' is not within the capabilities of human flesh; it is the gift of God. The 'world' (that is, humanity organised autonomously, without relation to God) 'cannot accept him (the Spirit of truth), because it neither sees him nor knows him' (John 14:17). And as soon as the Spirit enters a man or woman, he or she ceases to be part of the world, in that sense.

As Luther put it,

> 'nobody who has not the Spirit of God sees a jot of what is in the Scriptures. All men have their hearts darkened, so that, even when they can discuss and quote all that is in Scripture, they do not understand or really know any of it. They do not believe in God, nor do they believe that they are God's creatures, nor anything else... "The fool hath said in his heart, there is no God" (Ps. 14:1). The Spirit is needed for the understanding of all Scripture and every part of Scripture.'[12].

The point for us to grasp is this: the Spirit can only be given and received after Jesus has died on the Cross to pay the penalty for

---

12   Martin Luther, *The Bondage of the Will* (translated J. I. Packer and O. R. Johnston. London: James Clarke, 1957), p. 73f

human sin. John the Baptist cries out, 'Look, the Lamb of God, who takes away the sin of the world!' and then goes on to tell of the promise of God that, 'The man on whom you see the Spirit come down and remain is he who will baptise with the Holy Spirit' (John 1:29, 33). He will be able to 'baptise with the Holy Spirit', to pour the personal Spirit of God into the hearts of men and women when they are born again, only because He is also the Lamb who pays for sin.

This connection comes again in John 7. Back in chapter 4, Jesus has tantalisingly offered the Samaritan woman 'a spring of water welling up to eternal life' (John 4:14). Now in chapter 7 He makes the same offer to all:

> 'If anyone is thirsty, let him come to me and drink. Whoever believes in me, as the Scripture has said, streams of living water will flow from within him.' (John 7:37, 38).

John adds a very significant explanatory comment:

> 'By this he meant the Spirit, whom those who believed in him were later to receive. Up to that time the Spirit had not been given, since Jesus had not yet been glorified.' (John 7:39).

This is important. Some people – not very many, but some – had believed in Jesus. But they had not yet received the Spirit of God to live inside them. And they would not receive Him until Jesus 'had… been glorified'. In John's Gospel, Jesus is 'glorified' supremely when He is lifted up on the Cross to die. It is this death that makes it possible for the Spirit to be poured out. Of course, the Spirit existed before the Cross. He is God the eternal Holy Spirit. Of course, He was active before the Cross, in Creation, in equipping and inspiring the judges and prophets, and in giving faith to believers from Abraham onwards. None of that is new.

What is new is the depth, the permanence and the extent of His ministry. After the Cross He comes to dwell within every believer forever all over the world – his work is deeper, more lasting and more widespread. This ministry of the Spirit, this personal indwelling of God Himself, the apostles have not yet experienced, nor has Nicodemus, nor has the Samaritan woman, nor has anybody else before the Cross.

Why? I think the answer is this. We think it would be a wonderful thing if the Spirit of the living God could come into our hearts. But actually it would be suicide. For God's searching holiness and unapproachable light to enter my sinful heart would burn me up, until my sin is paid for. John Chrysostom got it right when he said,

> 'But why did the Spirit not come until Jesus departed? Because the curse was not yet taken away, sin was not yet loosed' – the burden taken off my back, like Christian in *The Pilgrim's Progress* – 'everything was still subject to the vengeance of God, and so he could not come.'[13]

The Spirit can only safely come into a cleansed and forgiven human heart. Paul expounds precisely this connection between the curse-bearing death of Jesus and the outpouring of the Spirit in Galatians 3:10-14.

> 'Christ redeemed us from the curse of the law by becoming a curse for us… *in order that* the blessing given to Abraham might come to the Gentiles through Christ Jesus, so that by faith we might receive the promise of the Spirit.' (Gal. 3:13, 14, my italics)

So we should thank God for the Cross, because were it not for the Cross the Spirit could not be given and we would remain in darkness, doomed like Lessing[14] to be endlessly seeking truth and never finding, fooling ourselves that we were enlightened when actually we walked in darkness. Until the Spirit came, nobody really understood anything, nobody repented and nobody

---

13 John Chrysostom, *Homilies on the Gospel of St. John* (Peabody, Massachusetts: Zondervan 'Nicene and Post-Nicene Fathers' Vol.14, 2004) ad loc.

14 See pp. 38-9.

believed. The Son of God Himself could preach His heart out day after day, speaking the very words of God, words that are spirit and life; and nobody believed. We need to learn from the failure of Jesus' earthly ministry to feel our utter dependence on the Cross and our daily dependence on the Spirit.

Jesus knew that His earthly ministry would be a failure. That failure did not take Jesus by surprise. This was why He Himself quoted those sobering words from Isaiah 6 about God closing people's eyes. He knew that His earthly ministry would be very like Isaiah's hard and unsuccessful ministry. He knew that only His death could make it possible for the Spirit to be poured out. And only when the Spirit was poured out would the divine words He spoke enter human hearts and change people from the inside, so that the Father truly would be made known.

When we try to speak of Jesus with others, and especially those of us who teach or preach the Bible, we need to remember our dependence upon the Spirit. If the Son of God Himself could not succeed before the Spirit was given, what chance have we?! We must never slip into thinking, 'Well, I have prepared carefully, so I guess God has got to bless.' 'I've had a good Bible training, so God is likely to bless.' 'I hold the office of Pastor or Minister, so God ought to bless.' 'They said I preached a good sermon last week, so God will probably bless this week as well.' None of this is true. God has not 'got' to do anything. The Spirit of God is the Sovereign God. Until and unless He chooses to come down from heaven and give new birth and new life, no one will grasp anything, no one will repent, no one will believe, no one will live a godly life, and no one will persevere as a Christian. We may not and must not presume on His grace, but must cry daily to Him for His sovereign gracious work.

The failure of Jesus' earthly ministry, and the weakness of His words before the Cross, were not unexpected. God knew, and Jesus knew, that this is how it must be. They do, however, serve as a powerful and sobering object lesson to us of the absolute necessity for a work of the Spirit in hearts, and the absolute necessity of the death of Jesus on the Cross, without which that Spirit could not be poured into hearts. Without the Cross, there would be no ministry of the Spirit in the believer; and without that ministry all would be darkness.

The great nineteenth-century Baptist preacher Charles Spurgeon wrote:

> 'The gospel is preached in the ears of all ...; it only comes with power to some. The power that is in the gospel does not lie in the eloquence of the preacher otherwise men would be converters of souls. Nor does it lie in the preacher's learning; otherwise it would consist of the wisdom of men. We might preach till our tongues rotted, till we should exhaust our lungs and die, but never a soul would be converted unless there were mysterious power going with it – the Holy Ghost changing the will of man. O Sirs! We might as well preach to stone walls as preach to humanity unless the Holy Ghost be with the word, to give it power to convert the soul.'[15]

Study and Discussion Questions

1. Read John 12:37-42. How does John sum up the effect of Jesus' earthly ministry?

2. Read through John 1–12 looking for the ways in which Jesus is described as elusive and in control.

3. Read through John 3, noting how Jesus (and John) highlight our inability to get ourselves up from the realm of this world into the realm of the Spirit.

4. Read through John 8:12-59. How do Jesus and John explain the hostility to Jesus? What has caused it?

5. Read the early chapters of Acts and contrast this with John 1–12. How are things different after the Cross, when the Spirit is poured out? Take some time to respond with wonder and adoration at how much more privileged we are than those who originally saw and heard Jesus physically on earth!

---

15   quoted in John R. W. Stott, *I believe in Preaching* (London: Hodder and Stoughton, 1982), p. 335

3

The Spirit, the Word
and His Apostles

So far we have considered two parallel and contrasting truths, both drawn from the first half of John's Gospel. On the one hand, we saw that the words of Jesus were the vehicle by which He made the Father known. It was His words which conveyed His teaching, interpreted His miracles and rendered His atoning death intelligible. We learned in that chapter how these words originated in the eternal life of Father and Son within the Trinity, and how these words were given again to Jesus in His earthly incarnation by the ministry of God the Holy Spirit who descended on Him and remained on Him, anointing and filling Him without limit. We thought with awe about the life-giving spiritual nature of those words, words that were spirit and life, and the words of eternal life.

On the other hand, we had to absorb the sober truth that until the Spirit was poured out, nobody really grasped the meaning of the wonderful words Jesus spoke. The Father was made visible, but nobody saw Him. We shall come back to that sober truth in chapters 6, 7 and the conclusion, to see how the ministry of the Spirit wonderfully addresses that blindness. But now we pick up the question with which we ended chapter 1:

where do we find Jesus' words and how can we hear His voice today? In this chapter and the next we explore the connection between the words of Jesus and the words of the Bible.

WHERE CAN WE HEAR JESUS' WORDS TODAY?

At the end of our study in chapter 1, we learned from John 12:44-50 about the enduring significance of Jesus' words after He left this earth[1]. This raises a huge question: where and how can we hear His words today? For Jesus is not here in bodily form to speak them, that we may hear them with the physical hearing of our ears.

This is a vital question, the answer to which has far-reaching ramifications. If we cannot answer it, then it is hard to see how Jesus' promise to go on and on making the Father known can be honoured. There are essentially only two kinds of answer we can give. Either we hear Jesus speaking in an interior and subjective way, or we hear Jesus speaking through the written and preached words of the Bible. There are variants of each of these, of course, and there are attempts to combine the two. But I believe that essentially they are distinct and incompatible answers. The latter is Christian and the former is pseudo-Christian.

To put it another way, the question is about the connection between Jesus the Eternal Word and the written words of the Bible. When we speak loosely of 'the word' there is this ambiguity. Do we mean the second person of the Trinity, the Eternal Word, Jesus Christ, or do we mean Scripture? Are we speaking of the Word who is a person, or of the Word that is words in a book?

At this point a division often appears between those who just assume that 'the Word' does mean Scripture (this being a generally untested assumption) and those who assume that 'the Word' means Jesus rather than the Bible (this assumption involves a generally unexamined doubt about Scripture). But

---

1   pp. 29-31

neither this untested assumption nor this unexamined doubt will suffice. We need to examine and test this connection. Doctrinally, it has been said that tying the doctrine of the Trinity to the doctrine of Scripture defines orthodox Christianity.[2]

There are many who wish to prise apart the Eternal Word and the scriptural words. So, for example, the Oxford scholar John Barton writes, 'it is not primarily the Bible that is the Word of God, but Jesus Christ.' We must not 'commit … bibliolatry: the elevation of the Bible above Christ himself… Christians are not those who believe in the Bible, but those who believe in Christ.'[3] Many church leaders have had the same said to them, perhaps less eloquently, but just as disconcertingly. How unsettling it is to be told that we are unspiritual for insisting on Bible teaching being at the heart of church life, or that by so doing we are substituting a dead book for the living experience of a Person. It sounds so pious when people say this to us. Who would not prefer a living person to printed words on a page? Who would want to be accused of worshipping a book? But I believe the accusation is unfounded and ultimately denies the power of the authentic Christ. The aim of this chapter and the next is to explore why.

I want to help us to resist this prising apart of the Word from the words. Our confidence in the Eternal Word is our confidence in the written words. I believe that every Bible word is spoken by the Eternal Word. I want to help you see why I believe this.

PRELIMINARY CLARIFICATIONS
We begin with two brief but necessary clarifications.

---

2   See Kevin J. Vanhoozer, 'Triune Discourse' in *Trinitarian Theology for the Church* (Daniel J. Trier and David Lauber (eds.)) (Nottingham: IVP/Apollos, 2009)

3   Timothy Ward, *Words of Life* (Nottingham: IVP, 2009), p. 12f

1. Red-letter Bibles are neither necessary nor helpful for finding the words of Jesus

The obvious – but wrong – answer to the question of where we find Jesus' words today is, 'Well, of course, we can read them in the red parts of a red-letter Bible!' But this is misleading, for at least three simple practical reasons.

First, the red words are not in the original language that Jesus spoke. They have been translated from Greek, and even the Greek is most unlikely to have been the exact words His spoke, since He seems, usually at least, to have taught in Aramaic. We know this from the few occasions when the precise Aramaic words have been preserved – 'Abba', 'Talitha koum', 'Eloi, Eloi, lama sabachthani'[4]. But apart from these, even if we read the New Testament in Greek, we cannot have access to the precise and actual words that Jesus spoke.

Second, there are no speech marks in the Greek manuscripts. Our translators – generally helpfully – add them in to make it easier for us to read. But there are times when we cannot tell when the direct speech of Jesus ends and the comments of one of the gospel-writers begins. The most famous of these is John 3:16-21. Jesus begins speaking in verse 10, and the context makes it clear that His direct speech continues at least to verse 15. But it is quite likely that verses 16-21 are the comment of John the gospel-writer rather than the direct speech of Jesus[5]. So we cannot even tell if the most famous verse in the Bible (John 3:16) was spoken by Jesus or by John!

Third, it is clear by comparing parallel passages, especially in Matthew, Mark and Luke, that the gospel-writers summarise and paraphrase what Jesus said (as well as putting it into Greek, as we have seen).[6]

---

4 Mark 14:36; 5:41; 15:34

5 This is the view of most commentators. For a concise summary of the reasons, see Andreas Köstenberger, *John* (Grand Rapids, Michigan: Baker Exegetical Commentary, 2004), p. 113f.

6 Compare, for example, Matthew 19:1-12 with Mark 10:1-12

The Spirit, the Word and His Apostles

For these three practical reasons, we do not and cannot have access – except in a few exceptional cases – to the precise words spoken by Jesus such as might in principle have been preserved by a voice recorder. Indeed, as we shall see, this is a good thing. For if we could, then our doctrine of Scripture would be essentially the same as the Muslim understanding of the Qur'an, and to read the Bible it would be essential to understand Hebrew, Aramaic and Greek. It would presumably also be forbidden to translate the Bible into any other language. One Muslim scholar asks precisely this question: 'Would Christian theology be willing to say that the discourse of Jesus Christ in Aramaic (and not Greek; *the distinction is important*) at a precise time and in a precise place on earth is related to God the Father as the Qur'anic discourse in Arabic transmitted by Muhammad is related to the Archetype [or "Mother"] of the Book retained in the presence of God transcendent?'[7] Happily for Christians, the answer is no. Christian theology has never shared with Muslim theology a 'dictation theory' of inspiration, that there is a divine 'Archetype' transmitted to a Prophet on earth and then recorded verbatim in a book. (This is, of course, why the Qur'an ought properly to be studied in Arabic and not in translation.)

So – paradoxically – red-letter Bibles encourage an understanding of the Bible that is more Muslim than Christian. It would be good if publishers ceased to print them. They certainly do not help us in our search to hear the words of Jesus Christ today. Happily, as we shall see in this chapter and chapter 4, we are able to hear the words of Jesus Christ with utter faithfulness in all the words of the New Testament, not just those printed in red.

.

---

7   Quoted in Telford Work, *Living and Active: Scripture in the Economy of Salvation* (Grand Rapids, Michigan: Eerdmans, 2002), p. 86 & n. 79, (Work's italics)

2. The words Logos and Rhēma are synonymous

The second preliminary clarification involves translation. There are two Greek words meaning 'word', *Logos* and *Rhēma*. It is sometimes claimed that these words have significantly different meanings, that *Logos* refers to the written or printed word in a book, and *Rhēma* to the immediate spoken word. So, it is suggested, the *Logos* of Jesus is found for us in the Bible; but what we also need to guide us is the immediate present-tense *Rhēma* of Jesus, spoken today by the mouth of the contemporary prophet. There are churches called 'Rhēma Churches' committed to this distinction and its theological implications for prophecy today. Sadly, they are building their identity and their theology on sand. Even if the two words may have subtly different nuances of meaning, a study of the New Testament's use of these words makes it clear that their meanings overlap so much as to be effectively synonymous.

In John's Gospel, for example, John has a well-known liking for using synonyms purely for the sake of stylistic variation and interest.[8] For example, he uses the words *Agapē* and *Philia* (and their associated verbs) as synonyms. He does the same with *Logos* and *Rhēma*. For example,

> 'He who belongs to God hears what God says. ['what God says' is literally 'the *rhēmata* – plural of *rhēma* – of God']' (John 8:47)

> 'He who does not love me will not obey my teaching [*logos*]. These words [plural of *logos*] you hear are not my own; they belong to the Father who sent me.' (John 14:24)

> 'For I gave them the words [plural of *rhēma*] you gave me…' (John 17:8)

Elsewhere in the New Testament we find the same interchangeable use of these two words. So it is not right to build

---

8   Leon Morris often draws attention to this in his commentary, *The Gospel according to John* (Revised Edition) (Grand Rapids, Michigan: Eerdmans New International Commentary on the New Testament, 1995).

a theology that sets the spoken word of the contemporary prophet alongside the written words of Scripture on this supposed distinction of meaning.

After those two necessary clarifications, we turn now to our serious constructive work, which will be in three stages. In this chapter we look at the link between Jesus and the apostles; then in the next chapter we move from the apostles to the New Testament; and finally, we ask about Jesus and the Old Testament.

JESUS AND APOSTOLIC TESTIMONY

We begin with a simple observation: if Jesus spoke words and Jesus is no longer here, then someone else needs to tell us what He said. That is to say, we are reliant upon testimony, the evidence of witnesses. This is the same in all human quests to know what a now-dead or absent person has said, after the event. Other people need to tell us, and the witnesses need to be trustworthy.

So let us consider the witnesses to Jesus. We shall do so in three stages. As we do, there is a degree of unavoidable logical circularity in our argument; for our only access to the Jesus whose testimony we are examining is via that same testimony. We shall mine the New Testament to build up our case for trusting the New Testament. This is not a problem unique to Christianity; it is the challenge that faces any historian. But it is not insuperable. For we can see, first, whether the story about the testimony hangs together in a coherent and persuasive way, and therefore, second, if we have reasonable grounds for trusting it. I hope we shall see that it does and we do.

1. *The apostles: their human preparation*

Luke tells us that after a whole night of prayer, Jesus 'called his disciples' (that is, the wider group of those following Him at the time) 'to him and chose twelve of them, whom he also designated apostles' (Luke 6:12, 13). This unique, hand-picked group are sometimes designated 'apostles' (particularly in Luke and Acts), sometimes 'the Twelve' (particularly in John), or 'his twelve disciples' (e.g. Matt. 10:1), and sometimes just 'the disciples' where the context makes it clear that it is specifically the apostles who are meant. The first characteristic we are to note is that Jesus chose them; they did not choose Him (unlike the traditional practice of a disciple choosing his rabbi). 'You did not choose me; but I chose you…' (John 15:16).

Jesus said to this group,

> 'you… must testify, for you have been with me from the beginning.' (John 15:27).

This was part of a very important pair of verses (John 15:26, 27), addressed to the eleven apostles (after Judas Iscariot had left) to which we shall return in chapters 6, 7 and the conclusion. For the moment we focus on two characteristics Jesus mentions. First, they had been 'with' Jesus. We find this also in Mark, where we read that Jesus,

> 'appointed twelve – designating them apostles – that they might be with him..' (Mark 3:14).

So an apostle had to be 'with' Jesus, watching and listening, a first-hand eye-witness and ear-witness of what Jesus said and did. They saw His miracles; they listened to His controversies with the Pharisees and other opponents; they heard His teaching; they engaged in question and answer with Him privately as well as hearing Him in public; they watched His life and behaviour. Not all of them saw every miracle or listened to every conversation. For example, only Peter, James and John saw the raising of Jairus's daughter (Mark 5:37-43). But between them they were with Him all the time.

Next, we need to note that they saw and heard it *all*. They were with Him 'from the beginning,' which does not mean His childhood, but the start of His public ministry at the time of John the Baptist's ministry and baptism, from the day when 'God anointed Jesus of Nazareth with the Holy Spirit and power' (Acts 10:38). When Peter led the disciples in choosing a replacement for Judas Iscariot, he set out the qualifications like this:

> 'Therefore it is necessary to choose one of the men who have been with us the whole time the Lord Jesus went in and out among us, beginning from John's baptism to the time when Jesus was taken up from us. For one of these must become a witness with us of his resurrection.' (Acts 1:21, 22).

To be an apostle it was not sufficient to have witnessed one of His resurrection appearances. Over 500 disciples had that privilege (1 Cor. 15:6). No, to be an apostle you had to 'have been with us', and therefore with Jesus, during the whole of His earthly ministry. For this was the revelation of the Father, this was the time during which He made the Father known. It is very important to note that there is a start point and an end point to this revelation; it was 'beginning from John's baptism' and it ended 'when Jesus was taken up from us'. Those three years or so were the complete and definitive revelation of the Father on earth. To be an apostle you had to have been there to see and hear it. In His great prayer just before He died, Jesus said to the Father (as we saw in the Introduction) that, 'I have revealed you *to those whom you gave me out of the world*', which in that context meant the apostles. He repeats this at the end of the prayer: 'I have made you known *to them*' (John 17:6, 26). Although He then promises to continue to make the Father known, the primary revelation was to that unique hand-picked band of eye-witnesses, who – between them – saw and heard the *whole* of the revelation in the earthly ministry, death and resurrection of Jesus Christ.

Finally, let us note that the apostolic testimony was plural. It was between them, as a group, that they gave their united testimony. While this does not prove anything, it strengthens our confidence that they are trustworthy.

So this was the human preparation Jesus ensured that they had. They were a hand-picked group of eye-witnesses of the whole of His earthly ministry, to be united in plural testimony. Jesus took great care over this preparation, for He knew it was going to be of the utmost importance after He had gone: 'And you also *must* testify, for you have been with me from the beginning' (John 15:27).

2. The apostles: their spiritual equipping
But it is more than that. It is not sufficient to have eye-witness testimony, even of this carefully-prepared, plural and safeguarded kind. What will happen when Jesus finally leaves them? After His resurrection and that wonderful 40 days of teaching (Acts 1:3), He ascends and the resurrection appearances cease. What happens then?

I suppose the easy answer is, 'they remember His teaching and teach it to others.' Would that it were so simple! But anyone who has studied even a modicum of history knows it is not. Eye-witnesses get things wrong; they misunderstand; they misconstrue. And even if eye-witnesses have perfect memories and make no mistakes in recall, the business of passing on the teaching of another person is far from simple. How can we be sure they have got it right, the balance, the thrust, the emphases, the nuances? How can they avoid saying they are teaching what Jesus taught, but actually just using 'Jesus' as a ventriloquist's doll, a cipher to say what they want to say, but carrying more authority? As one critic famously said of the nineteenth-century liberal Protestants looking at 'the life of Jesus', they looked down a deep well and what they saw was the reflection of their own ideas and selves. So how are we to hear the authentic voice of Jesus?

The answer lies in the spiritual provision Jesus made for the apostles. Speaking to His inner circle just before He died, Jesus said (John 14:24-6), 'He who does not love me will not obey my teaching. These words you hear are not my own; they belong to the Father who sent me.' So 'these words' or this 'teaching' is very, very important, for these are the words of the Father. These are the words by which the Father has been made known to them. 'All this I have spoken while still with you.' Yes, but what will happen when Jesus leaves them? How will the Father continue to be made known? The answer – wonderfully – follows immediately: 'But the Counsellor, the Holy Spirit, whom the Father will send in my name, will teach you all things and will remind you of everything I have said to you.'

This wonderful promise was made to the apostles. It could not be made to anyone else. Only the apostles could be reminded of what Jesus had said to them, because only the apostles were there to hear it all in the first place. The Holy Spirit cannot remind you and me of what the physical Jesus said to us during His earthly ministry, for we were not there to hear Him. But they were. And after He had gone, the Holy Spirit did just what Jesus had promised: He both taught them and reminded them. That is to say, He reminded them so that they remembered accurately, and He taught them so that they understood it correctly and could therefore teach it faithfully.

Again and again in John's Gospel we see the fruit of this work of the Spirit. In John 2, Jesus spoke of destroying and raising up the 'temple', and they didn't understand what He was talking about. But, 'After he was raised from the dead' – and therefore after the Cross, when He was glorified, and when the Spirit had come at Pentecost – 'his disciples recalled what he had said. Then they believed the Scripture and the words that Jesus had spoken' (John 2:22). The Holy Spirit enabled them both to remember and to understand what Jesus had said. Then again, when Jesus entered Jerusalem seated on a donkey, at the time 'his disciples did not understand all this'; they didn't understand in particular that this was in fulfilment of the prophecy of Zechariah 9 'Do not be afraid, O Daughter of Zion; see, your king is coming, seated on a donkey's colt' (John 12:15 quoting from Zech. 9:9). But, John continues, 'Only after Jesus was glorified' – and therefore when the Spirit was given (John 7:39) – 'did they realise that these things (i.e. Zech. 9) had been written about him and that they had done these things to him' (John 12:16). When He washed their feet, Jesus said, 'You do not realise now what I am doing, but later you will understand' (John 13:7). Of course, they understood that He was washing their feet; there were no prizes for grasping that! But they did not understand the significance of it, what it meant for His ministry of washing them, and what it would imply for how they related to one another, until afterwards, when the Spirit taught them. Even at the empty tomb, John writes that, 'They' – that is, Peter and the unnamed disciple, probably John himself – 'still did not understand from Scripture that Jesus had to rise from the dead' (John 20:9). Only when the Spirit came and taught them, did they grasp this. Again and again, the Spirit reminded them, and they remembered; the Spirit taught them, and they understood.

3. The apostles: their complete testimony to the completed revelation of the Father in Christ

We have seen that the apostles were eye-witnesses of the whole revelation of the Father through the words of Jesus Christ, and that the Holy Spirit reminded and taught them this revelation so that they remembered and understood it aright. This is wonderful. But there is more, and a deeper truth yet. In John 16:12-15 Jesus makes them another promise,

> 'I have much more to say to you, more than you can now bear. But when he, the Spirit of truth, comes, he will guide you into all truth. He will not speak on his own; he will speak only what he hears, and he will tell you what is yet to come. He will bring glory to me by taking from what is mine and making it known to you. All that belongs to the Father is mine. That is why I said the Spirit will take from what is mine and make it known to you.'

These verses begin with a puzzle: 'I have much more to say to you, more than you can now bear.' What does Jesus mean? Not long before, He had said to them,

The Spirit, the Word and His Apostles

> 'I no longer call you servants, because a servant does not know his master's business. Instead, I have called you friends, for everything that I learned from my Father I have made known to you.' (John 15:15).

Both passages are about 'making known', that is, 'making the Father known'. In John 15:15 Jesus draws a distinction between a servant who just does what he is told, whether or not he understands the rationale behind the instruction, and a friend, who is taken into the confidence of the other. Jesus says that the apostles are His friends and that 'everything' He has learned from the Father He has already 'made known' to them. By 'everything' He must mean everything there is to know of the Father that can be revealed, for Jesus knows the Father intimately, and has been 'in the bosom' of the Father from all eternity (John 1:18 KJV). He has held nothing back. He has not just given them the first instalment of an ongoing serial revelation of the Father; He has made the Father known to them. He has given them the full revelation of the Father.

So, given that He has already made known to them everything He has learned from the Father, what can He mean by saying that He has 'much more' to say to them? This is the puzzle. The point of John 15:15 is the open relationship of trust. Jesus doesn't hold back secret things from them and only give them the documents not marked 'top secret'. They have, as it were, the highest level of security clearance for access to God's truth. But although they have this security clearance (Jesus is open with them), they simply cannot cope with it all at once. They can't 'bear' it. It is too much and too heavy for them now. It is rather like when the Fraud Squad raid a company's offices, and we see them on television carrying out boxloads of papers and digital media, perhaps thousands or even millions of pages. In one sense, they have all the information from that day on. But they cannot 'bear' it yet, and it will take many months of unpacking and working through the material before they can issue their report. There is simply too much to absorb at once.

In a similar way, it is not that Jesus gradually gives the apostles more access to the revelation of the Father, rather as historians gradually get access to state papers under the 30-year rule. It is that the process of learning will take a lifetime and therefore they will need a lifetime tutor as they – as it were – work through the revelation of the Father in Jesus. It will not be sufficient for Jesus to give them some initial tuition and then leave them to get on with reading through the files, as it were. No, they will need a replacement tutor. And the Spirit is that lifetime tutor for the apostles.

So it is not that the Spirit will give extraneous spiritual material, things that are unrelated to what Jesus has already given them. No, what the Spirit does is gradually to unpack all that Jesus revealed to them, all they have seen in Him, all God has spoken to us by His Son. Hebrews 1:1, 2 makes the point that in the past there had been a gradual revelation, through the prophets at various times and in various ways; but now in Jesus God has spoken to us His final word. The Spirit does not add to the final word of Jesus; rather He unpacks that word for the apostles. He will not give them extra little presents of revelation arriving day by day in the heavenly hotline post, gradual downloads or updates (as we might get over the Internet for updating a programme); rather, He tutors them in the gradual unpacking of the one great present they have already been given.

It is important to be clear about this. When one commentator writes (commenting on John 16:12-15) that, 'The historical Jesus and his ministry stand *alongside* the ongoing living Jesus-in-Spirit, who is continuously experienced in the church'[9] (my italics), I think he implies that Jesus is promising new and supplementary revelations of the Father all down the history of the church. But this is not so, for Jesus has Himself given the sufficient and complete revelation of the Father. Any

---

9   Gary M. Burge, *John* (Grand Rapids, Michigan: Zondervan NIV Application Commentary, 2002), p. 439

suggestion of supplementary revelations of this fundamental kind inevitably detracts from the fullness and sufficiency of the Father being made known by Jesus Christ in history. Jesus Christ was not the start of a revelatory process; He was and is the revelatory event.

Jesus goes on to promise, 'But when he, the Spirit of truth, comes, he will guide you into all truth' (John 16:13). The word 'guide' comes from the same root as the word 'way' (as in John 14:6 'I am the Way…'). When He comes, He will 'way' you into all truth, lead you in the Way and the Truth. He will guide you to walk with and like Jesus. To be guided into truth is not primarily to be told facts. Truth in the New Testament is much deeper than knowing things, although it is never less. Truth is relationship with a person, the Lord Jesus who is the truth. To know the truth is to know the authentic Jesus and therefore to know the Father. Furthermore, truth is not merely something that is 'known' in a head-knowledge sense; truth is something which is done. I do not know truth so much as do truth. To be led into the truth is to be led into relationship with Jesus and to walk with Jesus, in His footsteps, to walk as He walked.

Now, in the first instance, this promise is given to the apostles, and it is very important to begin with this primary meaning. Jesus does not directly say to us or the church today, 'the Spirit will lead *you* into all truth.' He promised the apostles that the Spirit would lead *them* into all truth, just as in John 14:26 He reminds the apostles of all He had spoken, and teaches them what it means.

It is common to suggest that Jesus promises that the Holy Spirit will go on and on leading the church into more and more truth, in the sense of helping us to realise there have been things we have got wrong, and enabling us to get them right. The Jerusalem Council of Acts 15 is often suggested as a model for this. Acts 15 was a landmark in the history of the early church. The church agreed unitedly for the first time that Gentile believers in Christ would be admitted into Christ's church on the basis of faith alone, with no requirements to come under the Law of Moses. When sending their decision out from Jerusalem, the Council famously included the words, 'It seemed good to the Holy Spirit and to us ...' (Acts 15:28).

So, it is suggested, Synods and Councils of the church today may expect the same kind of leading. Indeed, they too may be able to preface their doctrinal or ethical novelties with the words, 'It has seemed good to the Holy Spirit and to us'. So, for example, the American pastor Rob Bell (famous for the Nooma videos and for his books) suggests that it is our responsibility to go on doing the kind of thing they did in Acts 15. The implications of this, he notes, 'are endless, serious and exhilarating'.[10] Well, they would certainly be endless, and – while it is shocking – it ought perhaps not surprise us that in his most recent book *Love Wins*, Bell leaves historic Christian orthodoxy well behind.[11] There would be no stability in Christian faith and no end to the changes and metamorphoses it would undergo.

But although helpful lessons may be learned from Acts 15 about Christian decision-making, the chapter is not a paradigm for church decisions today. It would be a serious mistake to think that a Synod or Council of the church today can make a change to Christian doctrine or ethics and preface it with the words, 'It has seemed good to the Holy Spirit and to us'. For this decision in Acts is part of the fulfilment of Jesus' promise to the *apostles* that the Holy Spirit would lead *them* into all truth, unpacking for them the complete revelation of the Father in Christ. The inclusion of the Gentiles was one very significant outworking of the great event of Jesus Christ. Paul repeatedly refers to it as 'the mystery of Christ' which had been hidden, but in the gospel is now revealed (e.g. Eph. 3:2, 3 and Col. 1:26). The Spirit revealed to Paul that the Gentile mission of the church was the necessary outworking of what Jesus Christ had done on earth. But when the apostolic era came to an end with

---

10   Rob Bell, *Velvet Elvis* (Grand Rapids, Michigan: Zondervan, 2005), p. 51

11   Rob Bell, *Love Wins*, (San Francisco: Collins, 2011). See also pp. 107-8.

the death of the last apostles, that ministry of the Spirit to the apostles was completed. He had indeed led the apostles into all truth, and we have that complete and sufficient deposit of truth in the apostolic collection we call the New Testament.

We shall consider in chapters 6 and 7, and the Conclusion, the implications of this promise for us today. For the moment, we focus on its primary meaning as a promise given to the apostles. This promise is strongly Trinitarian. Just as Jesus never spoke 'on his own,' that is, independently of the Father who sent him (e.g. John 7:16-18; 8:26, 28; 12:49; 14:10), so the Spirit 'will not speak on his own' but will speak 'only what he hears', that is, what He hears from the Father and the Son (John 16:13). His ministry is to lead the apostles into the full understanding of the completed revelation of the Father in the earthly life, teaching, miracles, death and resurrection of Jesus Christ.

But what does Jesus mean by saying, 'and he will tell you what is yet to come' (John 16:13)? Is this not a promise of future and additional revelations? Let us look closely at the argument. Unfortunately the NIV disguises a verbatim repetition between vv. 13 and 14):

'…he will tell you [literally, 'declare to you'] what is yet to come.'

'… taking from what is mine and making it known to you. [literally, "declare it to you"]'

The repetition of 'declare to you' strongly suggests that the subject of the first declaration, 'what is yet to come', is linked with the subject of the second declaration, 'what is mine'. Just as Jesus declared to the apostles the things of the Father, and so made the Father known, so the Spirit will declare to them the things of Jesus, and so make Jesus known, and therefore the Father known. Since 'all that belongs to the Father' belongs also to Jesus, when the Spirit takes the things of Jesus and makes them known, by doing so He simultaneously makes the Father known.

If so, then it would seem that the things that are 'yet to come' are in some way connected to the things of Jesus. They are the future implications of the things of Jesus. The Spirit is not promised to give them a kind of time-traveller insight into future events at random, in some simple predictive sense. He will teach them the implications of Jesus Christ for the future. This would include what it means to live under the New Covenant. For example, He taught them how Jews and Gentiles live together, all justified by faith alone (as the Spirit revealed to Peter in Acts 10). He showed them how the Temple is replaced and all the shadows and signs of OT Judaism are fulfilled in Jesus (as in Hebrews, for example). He revealed how Israel, the people of God, ceases to be a political kingdom and becomes an international church, Jew and Gentile (as in Matthew, Galatians or Romans, for example). He will teach them the implications of Christ's death and resurrection, looking forward to His second coming, the final judgement and His world lordship.

This is what we find, even in the book of Revelation, which is given 'to show (Christ's) servants what must soon take place' (Rev. 1:1) and yet consists not of simple predictions of the future, but rather (in apocalyptic style) of the unpacking of the implications of Christ for the present and future. Everything that results from, and is implied and caused by, the great event of the Word becoming flesh, the Spirit unpacked for the apostles over the years that followed. This is exactly what we find in the apostolic writings, not a random collection of predictive prophecies, but a coherent, Christ-centred, exposition of the past, the present and the future in the light of the revelation of the Father in Jesus Christ.

The Spirit 'will bring glory to' Jesus (John 16:14). Just as Jesus sought the Father's glory, so the Spirit seeks Jesus' glory. He takes the things of Jesus ('what is mine') – the grace and kindness of God given to us in and through Jesus – and makes them known, so that men and women may know Jesus, obey

Jesus, love Jesus, and worship Jesus. He is, if we may put it like this, the Person of the Trinity who most likes to remain invisible. He does not draw attention to His own ministry, but brings glory to Jesus, who makes the Father known.

And as He does that, all the intimacy of the Son and the Father are brought into play. What are the things of Jesus? They are the things that belong to the Father – all of them. All that belongs to the Father belongs to Jesus. The things of the Holy Spirit are without exception the things that belong to Jesus and therefore the things that belong to the Father (John 16:15).

CONCLUSION: JESUS EXPECTED THAT RESPONSE TO THE APOSTLES' TEACHING WOULD BE THE SAME AS RESPONSE TO HIS TEACHING

So we have seen that in the unique apostolic band we have a hand-picked group of men, prayerfully selected by Jesus to be with Him and to be eye-witnesses (between them) of the whole of His earthly ministry, death and resurrection. They were to see the Father made known. Further, He promised them a special and wonderful ministry of the Holy Spirit after Jesus' departure, by which they would be accurately reminded of the revelation they had seen, given a full and perceptive understanding of it, and led by the same Spirit into all the truth of Jesus. The purpose of this human preparation and divine provision was that the revelation of the Father in Jesus might be passed on to us in a way that is utterly trustworthy.

Jesus clearly expected that this is what would happen. He said to His apostles that,

> 'If they obeyed my teaching, they will obey yours also' (John 15:20).

Jesus says that response to the apostles' teaching is the same as response to His own teaching. He knew that when the time came for them to be on their own, their teaching would be His teaching, in its entirety and utter faithfulness, and that their words would precisely have the meaning and force of His words.

STUDY AND DISCUSSION QUESTIONS

1. Review the start of the chapter. Why does it matter so much that we discover where and how to hear Jesus' words today?

2. Review the distinction between Jesus the eternal Word and the Bible as the written word. Have you ever found this ambiguity confusing? Why?

3. What were the main features of the human preparation Jesus gave to His apostles and why was this human preparation insufficient on its own? What promise did Jesus make to remedy this insufficiency after His death?

4. Review the apparent contradiction between John 16:12 and John 15:15. How is it resolved?

5. Summarise our reasons for trusting the teaching of the apostles as the precise and faithful passing on of the words of Jesus.

4

The Spirit, the Word
and the Bible

We now consider the Bible as a whole. If Jesus perfectly revealed the Father, and the apostles reliably testified to Jesus in the power of the Spirit, then where does the Bible fit in? Does the Bible reveal the Father and, if so, how? We shall need to do this in two parts, for the Old Testament and the New Testament contribute in distinctive ways. We may perhaps sum this up by saying – at some risk of over-simplification – that the Old Testament is the testimony of the Father to the Son by the Spirit, and the New Testament is the testimony of the apostles by the Spirit to the Son (and so revealing the Father). If that sounds very Trinitarian, it is because it is!

APOSTOLIC TESTIMONY AND THE NEW TESTAMENT
In chapter 3 we have seen that Jesus made the Father known by His words, and that the words of the apostles in their teaching were precisely His words and His message, passed on with historical accuracy and spiritual precision and understanding. This was why the early church devoted themselves specifically to the teaching of the apostles, rather than to the teaching of other leaders within the wider group of disciples (Acts 2:42).

Indeed, the massive focus of miraculous activity on the apostles in the early years of the church[1] was intended by God precisely to validate their teaching ministry and encourage the church to trust that this unique band of men were indeed the bearers of the revelation of God in Christ (Heb. 2:3, 4; 2 Cor. 12:12).

But, in a sense, we seem only to have pushed the problem along a little. We have said that Jesus is not here, and so we must listen to the apostles. But the apostles are no longer here either. We cannot listen to them in any physical, audible sense. So how do we make the connection to the New Testament?

Someone has written that, 'No greater creative act can be mentioned in the whole history of the Church than the formation of the apostolic collection and the assigning to it of a position of equal rank with the Old Testament'.[2] It was indeed an extraordinary thing, that 400 or so years after the last Hebrew sacred writings were acknowledged as Scripture by the Jews, an entirely new collection of writings should be given equal scriptural status.

So how did this come to be? First, we should notice that John's Gospel claims to be the written testimony of the eye-witness apostle himself: 'This is the disciple who testifies to these things and *who wrote them down*' (John 21:24). It was recognised that the apostolic testimony needed to be written down. Whether a particular New Testament book was actually written by an apostle or not, what was written was part of the apostolic testimony. The New Testament is 'the apostolic collection'. Some were written by apostles. Others were written by those in the apostolic circle. For example, there is an early and probably reliable tradition that in the second Gospel Mark records the preaching of the apostle Peter. When Mark's Gospel began to circulate and be accepted, there were plenty of people

---

1   Although not all the miracles in Acts are done by the hands of the apostles, the great emphasis seems to be on this, from Acts 2:43 onwards, especially through Peter (in the first half) and Paul (in the second half).

2   Adolf von Harnack, quoted in Peter Adam, *Written for Us* (Nottingham: IVP, 2008), p. 225

alive who had heard the preaching of Peter. These people recognised that Mark's account was a trustworthy recording of that preaching. Luke tells us that he is recording the testimony of 'those who from the first were eye-witnesses and servants of the word,' which must primarily mean the apostles, although for his birth and infancy narrative it seems that Luke drew also on the testimony of Mary, the mother of Jesus. Those who read Luke and Acts recognised that Luke had indeed 'carefully investigated everything from the beginning' and written an account that gives us access to 'the certainty' of the gospel of Jesus (Luke 1:1-4).

Paul is well aware that his apostolic credentials are unusual, since he was not an eye-witness of the earthly ministry of Jesus, and only an eye-witness of His resurrection as 'one abnormally born' (1 Cor. 15:8), seeing the risen Jesus on the Damascus road well after the other resurrection appearances had ceased. But his message was exactly the same as the message of the other apostles (Gal. 2:2), and this precise and full harmony of message was acknowledged by the churches when they accepted his letters as Scripture.

Of course, all sorts of pious writings began to circulate in the early church, and we have access to a number of them. But the criterion for them to be recognised as Scripture and included later in the New Testament canon, was apostolicity, either authorship by an apostle directly or authorship by someone in the apostolic circle who was recognised as having faithfully recorded the apostolic teaching[3]. Those who recognised the trustworthiness of the documents now included in our New Testament were originally those who were contemporary with the apostles.

It is because the New Testament is the apostolic collection of writings, recorded by apostles or by others under the

---

3   C. E. Hill, *Who Chose the Gospels? Probing the Great Gospel Conspiracy* (Oxford University Press, 2010) is a careful historical study showing how the four canonical Gospels came to be accepted and others such as the Gospel of Judas and the Gospel of Thomas did not.

supervision of the Spirit, that we may confidently affirm and trust that every New Testament word is the word of Jesus, and therefore the word by which the Father is made known today. Jesus said He would continue to make the Father known; He does so by His words. We have those words, recorded with their exact force, meaning, balance and entirety, in the whole of the New Testament.

JESUS AND THE OLD TESTAMENT

But what of the Old Testament? The Old Testament is not in any simple or historical sense 'the words of Jesus'. Here it is necessary to come at the problem from a different angle, and to see the Old Testament as God the Father's testimony by God the Spirit to God the Son. It is a preparatory work, given by the Father through the inspiration of the Spirit, in order to prepare the way for the full revelation of the Father in Jesus the Son. The following six observations may be made.

1. Jesus quotes the Old Testament as the Word of God

First, Jesus repeatedly quotes from the Old Testament in a way that clearly indicates His glad acknowledgement that it is word for word the Word of God.[4] Perhaps the classic example of this is in Matthew 19, where Jesus says,

> 'at the beginning *the Creator* "made them male and female" (Gen. 1:27), and *said*, "For this reason a man will leave his father and mother and be united to his wife, and the two will become one flesh." (Gen. 2:24)' (Matt. 19:4, 5)

Notice how Jesus expresses it: '...the Creator...said...' the words quoted from Genesis 2:24. But in Genesis, this verse is not put explicitly into the mouth of God; it is just an explanatory comment by the human author. And yet Jesus says, 'the Creator...said...' these words. He regarded the interpretive comment of the human author as the precise words of God.

---

4   John Wenham, *Christ and the Bible* (Guildford, Surrey: Eagle, 1993) deals comprehensively with Jesus' view of the Old Testament.

Elsewhere Jesus quotes a Psalm as coming from the mouth of 'David, speaking by the Spirit' (Matt. 22:43). There are many other examples.

There is no reason to suppose that Jesus' ascription of divine inspiration to Old Testament texts was limited to the ones He explicitly quoted. Jesus shared with His Jewish contemporaries the conviction that every word of the sacred Scriptures was the Word of God. He had no hesitation in disagreeing with His contemporaries when He needed to; but in this case there was no need, for He fully shared this conviction with them. The one who speaks the words of God says that the Old Testament is the words of God.

2. Jesus Himself is shaped by the Old Testament in all His humanity
Second, Jesus' own humanity was shaped in every way by the Old Testament Scriptures. The Word became flesh, but the humanity He took upon Himself was Jewish in every way. As He grew through childhood, His prayers were Old Testament prayers (especially the Psalms), His worldview was a scriptural worldview, His categories of thought were scriptural categories, His worship of God was Old Testament worship, and His hopes were fashioned by the Old Testament. In every way His thinking, His affections and His feelings, His desires and His fears, were shaped by the Old Testament Scriptures. He thought in Old Testament language, as we see, for example, when He says to Nathanael, 'you shall see heaven open, and the angels of God ascending and descending on the Son of Man' (John 1:51). He could not have spoken like that had His thinking not been shaped by texts like Genesis 28 and Daniel 7.

3. Jesus fulfils the Old Testament: it sets His messianic agenda
Third, Jesus' whole ministry was shaped in general and in detail by the agenda of the Old Testament prophecies. Not only did He think in Old Testament categories, He acted in deliberate and conscious fulfilment of Old Testament prophecy. So, for example, He reads in Psalm 41 that, 'he who shared my bread

has lifted up his heel against me' (Ps. 41:9) and so 'to fulfil' this Scripture He gives the bread to Judas Iscariot (John 13:18, 26).

4. *The Old Testament is necessary to make Jesus intelligible*
Fourth, the Old Testament is essential to make Jesus intelligible.[5] Without it we would not understand any of the categories in which Jesus is presented to us. We would not know what 'the son of David' might mean, nor what 'the Son of Man' might signify, nor what Jesus meant by alluding to Himself in terms of 'Wisdom', nor as the one 'greater than the Temple' or 'greater than Solomon', nor as our Prophet, our High Priest, our Passover sacrifice, nor what 'Son of God' might mean. All these categories, so necessary to build up a picture of who Jesus claimed to be and who the apostles proclaimed Him to be, are Old Testament categories.

5. *Jesus is necessary to make the Old Testament intelligible*
What is more, Jesus Himself is necessary to make the Old Testament intelligible as a whole. There are so many things about the Old Testament that make no sense on their own, that seem to be reaching forward to some fulfilment beyond their day. To take just one example, Psalm 2 (together with Ps. 1 a programmatic start to the Psalter) proclaims that one day God's anointed King will reign over the whole world. You could perhaps sing that without too much of a sense of cognitive dissonance (of a disjunction between the song and the political reality) in the heyday of King Solomon, but what when the kingdom was divided, what when the northern kingdom was wiped off the map by Assyria, and what, supremely, when the southern kingdom was taken into exile in Babylon and there was no more king at all? And even after the exile, they continued to sing it long after there had been any king in David's line. That faith only made sense if one day the King of Psalm 2 would come. Again and again, the New Testament is the 'missing unity'

---

5   For points 2, 4 and 5 see Telford Work, *Living and Active: Scripture in the Economy of Salvation* (Grand Rapids, Michigan: Eerdmans, 2002), pp. 84-8, 167-78

of the Old Testament[6]. It is full of unfulfilled promises and until those promises find their 'yes' in Jesus Christ (2 Cor. 1:20), the Old Testament ends with a ragged collection of loose ends.

6. Jesus taught that the Old Testament is the Father's testimony to the Son
But the deepest and most significant connection between the Old Testament and Jesus is that it is the Father's own testimony to His Son. We see this most clearly in John 5:31-46, a section which focuses on the kinds of testimony that bear witness to Jesus. Jesus begins by claiming,

> 'If I testify about myself, my testimony is not valid. There is another who testifies in my favour, and I know that his testimony about me is valid' (John 5:31, 32)

Jesus is not a self-attested, autonomous, go-it-alone God making claims for Himself. He has a reliable witness to attest His genuineness. Jesus gradually builds up a picture of different witnesses until He comes to His climactic witness.

First, He speaks of John the Baptist, the last prophet of the Old Covenant era,

> 'You have sent to John (the Baptist) and he has testified to the truth. Not that I accept human testimony; but I mention it that you may be saved. John was a lamp that burned and gave light, and you chose for a time to enjoy his light' (John 5:33-35)

He reminds them that they had rejoiced in John the Baptist's popular ministry, and that John the Baptist had pointed them to Jesus[7]. But He goes on to say,

> 'I have testimony weightier than that of John. For the very work that the Father has given me to finish, and which I am doing, testifies that the Father has sent me' (John 5:36)

---

6   G. von Rad, quoted in Telford Work, *Living and Active: Scripture in the Economy of Salvation* (Grand Rapids, Michigan: Eerdmans, 2002), p. 168

7   See much of John 1

So Jesus' work – and supremely the work of the Cross – is evidence that He is who He said He was. But this is not all. The climax is the testimony of the Father himself:

> 'And the Father who sent me has himself testified concerning me. You have never heard his voice nor seen his form, nor does his word dwell in you, for you do not believe the one he sent. You diligently study the Scriptures because you think that by them you possess eternal life. These are the Scriptures that testify about me, yet you refuse to come to me to have life' (John 5:37-40)

The Father has given His testimony to Jesus in the Scriptures. When Jesus says 'nor does his word dwell in you' He may echo a sentiment like that of Psalm 119:11 ('I have hidden your word in my heart'). The problem with Jesus' opponents was that they had not hidden God's Word (the Old Testament Scriptures) in their hearts. This is why they had not heard His voice or seen His form; that is to say, they didn't really know God. Had they taken the Old Testament Scriptures into their hearts and really known the God of the Covenant, they would have recognised and believed in 'the one he sent.' John Chrysostom expresses the logic well when he paraphrases Jesus' words like this: '… if the scriptures everywhere say that it is necessary to give heed to Me, and yet ye believe not, it is quite clear that His word is removed from you.'[8]

They were right diligently to search the Scriptures. Those Scriptures did indeed point them to eternal life, and they did so by bearing witness about Jesus. In his book *Surprised by the Voice of God*, Jack Deere says that 'the religion of the Pharisees' was wrong because they 'preferred the Book over the living, speaking Word of God (John 5:36-47).'[9] But does this not misunderstand Jesus' argument? Jesus says that the Pharisees

---

8   John Chrysostom, *Homilies on the Gospel of St. John* (Peabody, Massachusetts: Zondervan, 'Nicene and Post-Nicene Fathers' Vol.14, 2004) ad loc.

9   Jack Deere, *Surprised by the Voice of God* (Grand Rapids, Michigan: Zondervan, 2006), p. 61

were right to search the Scriptures, but wrong not to see that these Scriptures were the Father's testimony to the Son (v. 39 and cf. v. 46). Jesus is not saying that the Old Testament is a dead book and they need His living voice; He is saying the Old Testament is a living divine book, but they haven't listened to it. Because, if they had, they would believe in Him.

A few verses later, Jesus reinforces this point by stressing that the first five books of the Bible, the Law of Moses, testify to Him:

> 'But do not think I will accuse you before the Father. Your accuser is Moses, on whom your hopes are set. If you believed Moses, you would believe me, for he wrote about me. But since you do not believe what he wrote, how are you going to believe what I say?' (John 5:45-47)

So, just as the New Testament is the Spirit's testimony to Jesus given by the ministry of the apostles, the Old Testament is the Father's testimony to Jesus, given by the ministry of the prophets. It was a wonderful privilege recently to preach in a synagogue now bought and used by the Chinese Church in London. For years the Hebrew Scriptures had been read in that building. But now at last when the building came into Christian use, we believe that those Scriptures were placed in their proper context and began to be understood aright.

The whole Bible is the word of Jesus and contributes together to the full and trustworthy testimony to the complete revelation of the Father in Jesus Christ. If we are going to print any of it in red, we should print it all!

THE DIFFERENCE BETWEEN THE OLD AND NEW TESTAMENTS
Christ is the final and complete revelation of the Father. He does not begin to make the Father known; He made the Father known. When He continues to make the Father known, He does not add anything to the revelation He has already given. Instead, He brings that same complete revelation into the life of men and women today. The letter to the Hebrews

expresses most succinctly this finality and its implications for the difference between the Old and New Testaments:

> 'In the past God spoke to our forefathers through the prophets at many times and in various ways, but in these last days he has spoken to us by his Son…' (Heb.1:1, 2)

The Old Testament is a gradual and shadowy unfolding of the shape of the Christ to come. It is the Father's testimony to the Son, given in advance so that those who have the Father's word within their hearts (that is, who understand and believe the Old Testament) will recognise and gladly receive the Son when He becomes flesh and lives among us.

This is exactly what a believer like Simeon does. In shadowy form, the Old Testament Scriptures have shown Simeon how to wait and what kind of Saviour to wait for. And so, when the Son comes he welcomes Him literally with open arms: 'Simeon took (Jesus) in his arms and praised God…' (Luke 2:28).

Peter writes about this:

> 'Concerning this salvation (the rescue that Christians experience), the prophets, who spoke of the grace that was to come to you, searched intently and with the greatest care, trying to find out the time and circumstances to which the Spirit of Christ in them was pointing when he predicted the sufferings of Christ and the glories that would follow.' (1 Pet. 1:10, 11)

The breath or Spirit of God, who is at the same time the Spirit of Christ, breathed in the Old Testament writers so that they knew in anticipation the shape of the Christ to come, that He must suffer and be glorified, even though they did not yet know exactly who He was and when He would come. The Old Testament, is therefore, a gradual unfolding, the curtain being as it were opened a crack, and then a wider crack, and then more and more, but always still partially obscured.

And then Christ came and made the Father known, so that those who saw Him had seen the Father. He is the full revelation of the Father, God's final Word. The New Testament has, therefore, a completely different character to the Old. It is the apostolic testimony to the complete revelation of the Father in Christ. It is the words that testify to the Final Word. It is the end of 'at many times and in various ways' (Heb. 1:1). Over the relatively short period of apostolic ministry (one generation, by contrast with many centuries for the Old Testament), God the Holy Spirit led the apostles into all the truth of Jesus, so that the New Testament is the complete and sufficient testimony to Jesus who is Himself the complete and sufficient revelation of the Father. It follows that the New Testament is not a continuation of the Old Testament, such that we may expect even newer testaments to follow; it is the culmination, the climax, the conclusion of the Old Testament. After this we need no further revelations, for God has spoken His final Word.

There is, therefore, a distinction between the rationale behind the formation of the Old Testament canon and the rationale behind the formation of the New Testament canon. For what came to be known as the Old Testament (the 'holy Scriptures' for example in 2 Tim. 3:15), the list or canon was closed when it was perceived that prophecy had ceased, perhaps about 400 years before Christ. In a sense, the Old Testament petered out; it was a lot of loose ends, unfinished, waiting, waiting, waiting, for someone. The books of the Old Testament came together gradually, being written over a period of many centuries.

But for the New Testament it was very different. The New Testament exploded into existence, in historical terms. It is the complete testimony to one great climactic revelatory event, God's final Word. It was written over a very short time indeed, just a few decades. Although the precise list of books recognised as New Testament Scripture took a few centuries to be finalised in all its detail, the principle that this collection is the finite and never-to-be-added-to deposit of the apostolic teaching was evident from very early on. It is true that there was debate about a few of the less-central books for a while. But nobody after the apostolic period would be able to write something and see it incorporated into the New Testament canon.

N. T. Wright's five-act model

This is an appropriate point to comment on the five-act model for the Bible and the church suggested and popularised by the distinguished New Testament scholar N. T. Wright. In his book *The New Testament and the People of God*, Wright argues that the best way to think about the Bible is in terms of story or narrative. 'Worldviews', he says, 'provide the *stories* through which human beings view reality. Narrative is the most characteristic expression of worldview…' Both the grand overarching story and the individual stories of the Bible communicate to us the worldview of God and thereby shape our thinking and our behaviour. He asks us 'to consider how stories might carry, or be vehicles for, authority' that is, how they may effectively shape us.[10]

It is worth quoting at length the suggestion he then makes:

'Suppose there exists a Shakespeare play, most of whose fifth act has been lost. The first four acts provide, let us suppose, such a remarkable wealth of characterization, such a crescendo of excitement within the plot, that it is generally agreed that the play ought to be staged. Nevertheless, it is felt inappropriate actually to write a fifth act once and for all: it would freeze the play into one form, and commit Shakespeare as it were to being prospectively responsible for a work not in fact his own. Better, it might be felt, to give the key parts to trained, sensitive and experienced Shakespearian actors, who would immerse themselves in the first four acts, and in the language and culture of Shakespeare and his time, *and who would then be told to work out a fifth act for themselves.*

10   N. T. Wright, *The New Testament and the People of God* (London: SPCK, 1992), pp. 123, 140

'Consider the result. The first four acts, existing as they did, would be the undoubted 'authority' for the task in hand. That is, anyone could properly object to the new improvisation on the grounds that some character was now behaving inconsistently, or that some sub-plot or theme, adumbrated earlier, had not reached its proper resolution. This 'authority' of the first four acts would not consist – could not consist! – in an implicit command that the actors should repeat the earlier parts of the play over and over again. It would consist in the face of an as yet unfinished drama, containing its own impetus and forward movement, which demanded to be concluded in an appropriate manner. It would require of the actors a free and responsible entering into the story as it stood, in order first to understand how the threads could appropriately be drawn together and then to put that understanding into effect by speaking and acting with both innovation and consistency. This model could and perhaps should be adapted further: it offers quite a range of possibilities.'[11]

Wright goes on to suggest that we might see the biblical story as consisting of five acts:

'1-Creation; 2-Fall; 3-Israel; 4-Jesus. The writing of the New Testament – including the writing of the gospels – would then form the first scene in the fifth act, and would simultaneously give hints (Rom. 8, 1 Cor. 15, parts of the Apocalypse) of how the play is supposed to end.'[12]

Although this was written in 1992, Wright has persevered with this five-act model and popularised it in his 2005 work *The Last Word: Beyond the Bible Wars to a New Understanding of the Authority of Scripture*.[13] It is an attractive and suggestive analogy. But it is

---

11   Ibid., p. 140

12   Ibid., p. 141f

13   N. T. Wright, *The Last Word: Beyond the Bible Wars to a New Understanding of the Authority of Scripture* (San Francisco: HarperCollins, 2005), pp. 121-42; the book was also published in the UK as *Scripture and the Authority of God* (London: SPCK, 2005)

not an analogy drawn from Scripture itself, and there is a real danger that in its use, this vivid metaphorical tail will end up wagging the biblical dog. In the end I believe it is misleading and ultimately very dangerous, for two reasons.

First, it is ambiguous. Wright carefully nuances his use of the analogy by saying, for example, that Act 4 (Jesus) is 'the foundation upon which our present (fifth) act is based' and, 'the New Testament is the foundation charter of the fifth act'. Indeed, because the New Testament includes the start of Act 5, it follows that, 'We who call ourselves Christians must be totally committed to telling the story of Jesus both as the climax of Israel's story and as the foundation of our own. We recognise ourselves as the direct successors of the churches of Corinth, Ephesus and the rest, and we need to pay attention to what was said to them as though it was said to us'. This is strong and helpful so far as it goes.

Nevertheless, the analogy is intended by Wright to imply both continuity *and discontinuity*, so that, 'We must be ferociously loyal to what has gone before and cheerfully open about what must come next' expecting that in the present moment, 'genuinely new things can and do happen'. Indeed, when this model is followed, 'all kinds of opportunities will arise for fresh words to be spoken, illuminating the passages that have been heard and reverberating with them, but also moving forward to suggest what fresh meanings they might bear for today and tomorrow'.[14] It is not clear whether this genuine newness is intended to extend to developments in doctrine (perhaps analogous to the 'redemptive trajectory' idea we shall meet later[15]) or simply to be the reapplication of a definitive revelation to new situations.

It is perhaps symptomatic of this ambiguity that the American edition of *The Last Word* comes with warm commendations on the back from Brian McLaren, who seems

---

14   Ibid., pp. 123-25, 133

15   See p. 105

open to new developments of *doctrine[16]*, and J.I. Packer, who is not. Although Wright himself is orthodox in accepting the biblical canon, his model inevitably weakens the significance of the canon as the closed and definitive basis for Christianity, and plays into the hands of those who wish to question and downplay the importance of the canon. But the canon is the expression in church history of the grand theological finality of the revelation of the Father in Jesus Christ. If we sideline it, whether deliberately or inadvertently, we begin to marginalise Christ.

My second reason for questioning this model of biblical authority is that it seems to me that it overplays the category of narrative for understanding the Bible. The Bible certainly does tell a great overarching story, and in so doing it tells countless other smaller stories. But I want to suggest that the category of testimony is perhaps a more central and definitive category than narrative, when we are considering the whole Bible: the Bible is not so much an ongoing and developing story, of which we are performing the final act, as the definitive testimony to the revelation of the invisible Father God through Jesus Christ. Or, to nuance this, we might say that the Bible is a *completed* narrative. It is a story which bears testimony to a completed revelation, not a story which is going on being written. Of course, the story of God's rescue actions in history continues to be written; but the story of the Father's revelation in Christ has been completed and fully and reliably attested in the Bible.

So the Old Testament is the developing and gradually unfolding testimony of the Father by the Spirit to the Son, and the New Testament is the complete and sufficient testimony of the Spirit through the apostles to the Son. Together they do not just tell us Acts 1-4 of a five-act drama. They give us the complete and authoritative testimony to Jesus, God's Final Word, and call us to submit to Him with the obedience of faith, as He is revealed in the Bible.

16   Brian McLaren, *A New Kind of Christianity* (London: Hodder & Stoughton, 2010)

MANUSCRIPTS AND TRANSLATIONS

We need, of course, to put in the usual qualification, that the full and perfect revelation of the Father through accurate life-giving testimony to Jesus, is given in the Bible words in their original manuscripts in the original languages. Since we do not have access to any of the original manuscripts, this means that the scholarly work of what is called 'textual criticism' is necessary. Textual criticism is the discipline of examining all the manuscripts we do have and working back from those to the best approximation we can manage to the wording of the original manuscripts. It is an honourable skill and one that has been well-honed over the years.[17] Thank God we have excellent and strong manuscript evidence and that it is not difficult to be very confident indeed about the very large majority of the Bible's words. No Christian doctrine depends on those parts where there are residual uncertainties.

Likewise, the translation of the Bible into other languages is an honourable and demanding skill. We should thank God for trustworthy and skilled scholars who give us access to reliable translations. No translation is perfect. But there are – in English, at any rate – a number of very reliable translations, so that no-one need be anxious that they do not have substantial and sufficient access to the words of God.

CONCLUSION

We began chapter 3 by asking where we can find and hear Jesus' words today, those wonderful words that make the Father known, that are spirit and life, the words of eternal life. We have seen that the New Testament is the reliable apostolic testimony to Jesus and His words, and that the Old Testament is the Father's testimony to prepare the way for Jesus. In this

---

17   The introduction to Bruce M. Metzger, *A Textual Commentary on the Greek New Testament* (3rd Edition). (Stuttgart: United Bible Societies, 1975) gives a clear introduction to the principles for New Testament textual criticism. For the Old Testament, see Ellis R. Brotzman, *Old Testament Textual Criticism* (Grand Rapids, Michigan: Baker, 1994)

deeply Trinitarian way the Father and the Son cooperate in the revelation of God. The Father gives a reliable and gradually growing shadowy revelation that points forward to the climactic revelation by which He will be fully made known by the Son.

We conclude joyfully by affirming that we have good and coherent reasons for believing that we have the revelation of the Father today in every word of the complete Bible testimony to Christ. We can look those in the eye who want to drive a wedge between Jesus, the Eternal Word, and the written words of Scripture and affirm with confidence that we know the One precisely through the other. The doctrine of Scripture is indeed integral to the doctrine of the Trinity. The Word and His words are inseparable.

STUDY AND DISCUSSION QUESTIONS

1. What indications do we have that great care and trouble was taken to write down the teaching of the apostles in a reliable form?

2. Give a summary of the reasons why we may reasonably trust that the New Testament reliably gives us the teaching of the apostles.

3. Summarise in your own words each of the reasons given for trusting that the Old Testament is the trustworthy Word of God, and therefore part of the words of the eternal Word. Which do you think is the strongest reason, and why?

4. Both the Old and the New Testament have a canon, a fixed list of books. What is the difference between the reasoning that lies behind the Old Testament canon and the theology that lies behind the closure of the New Testament canon?

5. Summarise the five-act model outlined on p 78-81. In this model, how does the Bible exercise authority in the church? What is ambiguous about this model and what are its weaknesses?

6. How would you answer a Muslim critic who says, 'Your Christian Scriptures are corrupt. They have been changed over the centuries, unlike the Qur'an'?

5

The Spirit
and understanding the Bible

So far in our study we have thought about the wonderful truth
that Jesus Christ made the Father God known. In chapter 1 we
saw that He made the Father known by His words. In chapter 2
we learned the sober truth that it was only after the Cross, when
the Spirit could be poured into human hearts, that men and
women began really to understand those words and to respond
with faith. Chapters 3 and 4 asked the question where we may
find and hear the words of Jesus Christ today. We built our case
for trusting that His words are precisely Bible words, that the
whole Bible is the reliable testimony of and to Jesus Christ, and
therefore the means by which Jesus Christ continues to make
the Father known today.

But can we understand the Bible? Is the Bible able – or,
to be precise, is God able through the Bible – to make the
Father known to us today? 'It's all a matter of interpretation,'
people say. 'You can make the Bible mean just what you want
it to mean.' 'Why should your interpretation of the Bible be
any better than my interpretation?' 'What do we do when our
interpretations differ? Can we happily affirm them both as true
– one true for you and another true for me? If not, what are

we to do?' This is very important. If we cannot understand the Bible as revealing to us objective truth, there is no way that we will have the objective Father God made known to us through it. It is, therefore, very important that we have confidence that the Bible can be understood, that it can really and objectively make known to us the invisible Father God.

THE PROBLEM OF BIBLE INTERPRETATION

The technical term for the study of interpretation is hermeneutics, a word taken from the Greek word for interpreting. Hermeneutics has become something of a growth industry in the academic worlds of philosophy and literary criticism, and particularly in the fields of Christian biblical studies and theology.[1] Some of us may be tempted to dismiss the whole subject out of hand, and just fall back on 'what the Bible says and obviously means'. Before we take that deceptively easy way out, I want to persuade you that there is a problem to be grappled with, not just academically, but practically and pastorally.

In most churches people fall back on two equally unsatisfactory strategies (if we can dignify them with that name): anarchy and tyranny. One common way of interpreting the Bible (for example, in church Bible study groups) is anarchy. And the instinctive response of some church leaders is tyranny.

---

1   . In writing this chapter I have been most helped by the following three books: Kevin J. Vanhoozer, *Is there a meaning in this text?* (Leicester: IVP/Apollos, 1998) is a clear but technical study of many of the issues. I found it very helpful and it repaid careful study. Many of the ideas in this chapter are taken from Vanhoozer. Graeme Goldsworthy, *Gospel-centred Hermeneutics* (Nottingham: IVP/Apollos, 2006) is strong on the centrality of Christ and on Christ as the interpreter of meaning. Mark D. Thompson, *A Clear and Present Word* (New Studies in Biblical Theology, Nottingham: IVP/Apollos, 2006) is a comprehensive and (appropriately) clear study of the clarity or perspicuity of Scripture. I have tried to avoid the technical jargon so far as possible in the main text of the chapter. In addition, A. C. Thiselton, *New Horizons in Hermeneutics* (London: HarperCollins, 1992) includes comprehensive discussion of most of the key scholarly contributors to the debates.

The Spirit and understanding the Bible

Anarchy is where everyone understands the Bible in a way that is right in their own eyes. The Bible text becomes a mirror in which we see only ourselves and our existing prejudices, or an echo chamber in which we hear the sound of our own voices. Many of us have sat in Bible studies where we pretty much know what each person will say. You can almost write the script. There are no surprises, no challenges and no signs of real personal change. The text functions as a ventriloquist's dummy. It is an occasion for the Bible readers to hear themselves speak and reinforce their own prejudices. In Albert Schweitzer's famous analogy, they look down a deep well and discover the reflections of their own faces at the bottom.[2]

Anarchy is when, in a Bible study group, two people say contradictory things about how they understand the passage, and the group smile, have another cup of tea and carry on as though they are both right. This really will not do. In our heart of hearts, none of us really believes that meaning lies entirely in the imagination of the individual reader. In 2007 *The Guardian* ran a poster advertising campaign, with the words,

Opinions are not facts.

What happened

and how you feel about it

are two different things.

And people should know

which is which.

How right they were. Anarchy will not do. But if we cannot live with anarchy, what are we to do, in a Bible study group, a church council or a pulpit? The classic answer in church history is tyranny. If we do not want interpretive chaos, we

---

2   Schweitzer used this analogy of the nineteenth-century liberal Protestant so-called Quests for the Historical Jesus. The 'Jesuses' they came up with were pale reflections of themselves.

must move to interpretive dogmatism: there is only one correct meaning, and I/we have it. If the interpreters have no king, they need some kind of a Pope to tell them what it means.

This is the response of the Church of Rome during the Reformation. The Fourth Session of the Council of Trent (1546) decreed, '...in order to restrain irresponsible minds, that no one shall presume in matters of faith or morals [pertaining to the edification for Christian doctrine] to rely on his own conceptions to turn Scripture to his own meaning, contrary to the meaning that Holy Mother Church has held and holds – for it belongs to her to judge the true sense and interpretation of Holy Scripture.' It is the task of the church 'to determine the true sense and interpretation of Holy Scriptures'.[3]

Before disagreeing with this, Protestants need to try to understand sympathetically why they said this. Two student friends were discussing this, one a Roman Catholic, the other an evangelical Protestant. The Roman Catholic asked his priest for advice and help in these discussions, and this is some of what he said. He asked the priest why – as he had noticed – Protestants seemed to know their Bibles better than Catholics. To which the priest replied, 'An irreverent answer might be that indeed Protestants follow the Bible more closely than Catholics, which is exactly why it sometimes seems that no two Protestants have precisely the same beliefs. Indeed "Sola Scriptura" is an heretical and dangerous principle, which is at the root of almost everything which is wrong and dangerous about Protestantism.' Dangerous, that is, because it leads to anarchy. So, says the priest, ask your Protestant friend, 'if the Bible is all that one needs, why is it that there are literally thousands of sects with widely varying beliefs, all of whom proclaim themselves to be Bible-based?'

It is a fair question. We are vulnerable to the accusation that we are endlessly fissiparous, always splitting and dividing. So

---

3   Kevin J. Vanhoozer, *Is there a meaning in this text?* (Leicester: IVP/Apollos, 1998), p. 171

how are we to prevent the Balkanization, the disintegration of Protestantism or Evangelicalism? Do we have to fall back on a Protestant Pope, a scholar, a conference speaker, a charismatic leader, a guru, who will tell us how to interpret because, as it were, they have the power of the microphone?

As Graeme Goldsworthy points out, sometimes in evangelicalism, when we disagree amongst ourselves, 'Suddenly the clarity of Scripture seems to mean, "It's quite clear to me: why can't you see what is obvious?"'[4]! Speaking of some American Fundamentalism, Vanhoozer makes the point that 'Fundamentalism... preaches the authority of the text but practices the authority of the interpretive community'. That is, in theory the Bible rules. But in practice, powerful people within the community tell us 'what the Bible means'.

A friend observed to me, when we were discussing this, how quickly and unstably a group can switch from anarchy to tyranny. One moment everyone says something different. The next moment some powerful character asserts one interpretation as true, and they all fall over like ninepins before the force of his personality.

But neither anarchy nor tyranny is satisfactory. I have spent some time on this because I want us to feel the seriousness of the challenge. My guess is that in some of our circles we are conscious of the dangers of anarchy. We have spent too long in Bible studies where the text 'means' something to one person and something contradictory to another, and everyone sits around drinking coffee and smiling. And so our danger is that we will instinctively move towards interpretive tyranny as the only practical way to keep order in church. I think we see this in the desire to have a guru, an expert, someone to whom we habitually turn for 'the answer'. One of the strange experiences that greeted me when I began leading

4   Graeme Goldsworthy, *Gospel-centred Hermeneutics* (Nottingham: IVP/Apollos, 2006), p. 24

a Bible training course was that quite suddenly – and for no good reason! – I found myself cast in that role. 'Let's ask Christopher,' they began to say, as though Christopher will be able to give the answer *ex cathedra*. Indeed one of our students was on holiday in Rome and sent me a postcard of the Pope, on the back of which she had written the words, 'Saw this, and thought of you!' She was being mischievous, for both she and I know that Bible teachers ought never to set themselves up as interpretive authorities.

So in this chapter we are going to explore some foundational principles which can guide us as we seek to understand the Bible together. One of my aims is to help us intercept interpretive tyranny when it tries to gatecrash the party dressed up as the authority of the text. What is at stake is the possibility that the church can be reformed by the Word of God, that the Word of God will speak from outside to change us. So the stakes are high. If we cannot go the way of anarchy and we must not go the way of tyranny, where ought we to go?[5]

So although, when we feel mired in the complexities of the hermeneutics industry, we may be tempted to pronounce a plague on all their houses, and to retreat into old certainties or common sense, we cannot avoid interpretation. Whether or not we think of ourselves as Bible interpreters, we cannot read or teach the Bible without doing interpretation. It is better to interpret in a way that is examined and thoughtful than to interpret while denying that we are interpreting.

Our argument will develop as follows. First, we shall ask what is the goal of Bible interpretation. Then we will look at the implications for understanding the Bible of (a) its character as testimony to Christ, (b) its completeness as testimony to Christ, and (c) its clarity as testimony to Christ.

---

5   Vanhoozer asks, "Is there an alternative to hermeneutic anarchy, where everyone does what is right in his or her own eyes, and hermeneutic totalitarianism, where the individual's beliefs are governed by institutional powers?" Kevin J. Vanhoozer, *Is there a meaning in this text?* (Leicester: IVP/Apollos, 1998), p. 27

The Spirit and understanding the Bible

THE GOAL OF BIBLE INTERPRETATION

Let us ask first, what is the aim and purpose of understanding the Bible? Vanhoozer retells a parable told by the Danish theologian Soren Kierkegaard.[6] It is called 'the parable of the King's decree'. Imagine a country, says Kierkegaard, in which the King issues a decree. But instead of complying with the decree the King's subjects begin to interpret it. Each new day sees new interpretations. It means this…or this… or that. Soon the population can hardly keep track of the varied interpretations on offer. Everything is interpretation – but no one reads the decree in such a way that he does what it says. Indeed, says Kierkegaard of much of the hermeneutics industry of his day, 'Look more closely and you will see that its purpose is to defend itself against God's Word.'

Let me express this in terms of the theme of this book. The aim of the Bible, I have argued, is to make the Father known. There is a real, objective, substantial, invisible Father God. By nature we do not know Him as Father[7]. Jesus made Him known by His words and deeds interpreted by words. He entrusted those words to His apostles. He affirmed that the Old Testament is an integral part of those words. The whole Bible is, word for word, the revelation of the Father through Jesus. We need, therefore, to read the Bible in line with this central purpose and aim.

It has been said that there are three ways in which people read the Bible. Some read it as a mirror; it simply reflects back to them their own prejudices and preconceptions. They are unchanged by it. The result is interpretive anarchy. Others read it the way we might view a painting in a gallery; they focus all their attention on the text. They analyse the text, they discuss the text, but they never see the one to whom the text testifies. (We

---

6   Ibid., p. 16

7   Although we know enough of His 'godness' to make us guilty for not worshipping Him. (Rom. 1:18-20)

saw in chapter 4 that this was the problem of the Pharisees[8]). The result is an arid Pharisaism. Instead, we ought to read the Bible more like the way we look through a window; our goal is to see the one whom the window opens to us. As we hear the words of Jesus Christ in the whole Bible, He makes the Father known to us. The goal of Bible interpretation is that we should walk in fellowship with the Father and the Son (1 John 1:3).

THE CHARACTER OF THE BIBLE AS TESTIMONY TO CHRIST

Second, let us explore the implications of our argument so far in chapters 1-4. We have seen that Christ makes the Father known through His words, and that those words are reliably found for us in Bible words. It follows that the centre, focus and unifying theme of the Bible is Christ, and therefore the Father, since it is Christ who makes the Father known. This has enormous implications for understanding the Bible. If we do not grasp this we are bound to misread the Bible, rather as we will inevitably misread a biography of a Formula One driver if we think it is a car maintenance manual.

Brian McLaren: the Bible as cultural library

Brian McLaren is a prominent leader in the so-called Emerging (or Emergent) Church movement. In his book *A New Kind of Christianity*, McLaren contrasts the idea of the Bible as a written constitution (fixed, authoritative and definitive) with his preferred model of the Bible as 'the library of a culture and community – the culture and community of people who trace their history back to Abraham, Isaac and Jacob'.

For him, what unifies the Bible library is not any answers that may be suggested, but the fact that this stream of historical culture argue about the same *questions*. A culture, including the Bible culture, is people who 'propose a variety of answers to the same basic questions'. Belonging to this culture means you agree that these questions, and not others, are the really

8   See pp. 74-5, discussion of John 5:37-40

important questions, 'whatever answers you prefer or propose'. The Bible library 'preserves, presents and inspires an ongoing vigorous conversation with and about God, a living and vital civil argument into which we are all invited *and through which God is revealed*' (my italics). [9] Sadly, this misses the central claim of the Christian faith, that the Father has been made known by Jesus Christ. He is not revealed by a conversation, but by a Person. And the Bible is the coherent and consistent testimony to the words of that Person.

In preparing this book I have read a number of books by people whose doctrine of Scripture has developed from an inherited high evangelical understanding to something less clearly authoritative. And one of the features I have noticed in at least some of them is that they do not seem to have (or have had?) a clear understanding of the Bible as the testimony to Christ. So, for example, both Jack Deere and Joyce Huggett have written books about how God speaks today; [10] but in neither of them does there seem to be a clear grasp of the unique, comprehensive and unrepeatable revelation of the Father in Christ, and how the Bible gives us this revelation. As soon as we lose this framework of understanding, the Bible quickly becomes just one resource among many others for hearing God speak.

Christ as the mediator of meaning
The Gospels record that at the Transfiguration the voice from heaven told the disciples to listen to Jesus Christ (Luke 9:35). This command is heavily freighted with meaning and significance. For as they reflected later on the person and meaning of Christ, the apostles were gradually guided by the Spirit to understand that he was and is the mediator between God and human beings,

---

9   Brian McLaren, *A New Kind of Christianity* (London: Hodder & Stoughton, 2010), pp. 105-9

10   Jack Deere, *Surprised by the Voice of God* (Grand Rapids, Michigan: Zondervan, 2006) and Joyce Huggett, *Listening to God* (2nd Edition, London: Hodder & Stoughton, 1996)

that He is the principle of coherence in the universe, the one in whom the universe holds together, and the one in whom are all the treasures of wisdom and knowledge (1 Tim. 2:5; Col. 1:16; Eph. 1:9, 10; Col. 2:2, 3).

In a very deep sense, therefore, He is the interpretive key to the universe. Only when we listen to Him do the scales begin to fall from our eyes. Ultimately the reason for this is that He makes the Father known, and the Father is the source of meaning in the universe. To be somewhat philosophical for a moment, let us think about this business of meaning. Literary critics have recognised that when they say there is no objective meaning, that a text cannot actually and in a stable way *mean* anything, what they are actually saying is that there is no objective God. It has been said that the nineteenth century proclaimed the death of God, and then – as a consequence – the twentieth century proclaimed the death of meaning. As one critic has put it, 'The death of God was the disappearance of the Author who had inscribed absolute truth and univocal meaning in world history and human experience' (Mark Taylor). Roland Barthes says that the refusal to assign a fixed meaning either to the world or to texts 'liberates an activity we may call countertheological, properly revolutionary, *for to refuse to halt meaning[11] is finally to refuse God*'. In his book *Real Presences* George Steiner writes: '[This essay] proposes that any coherent understanding of what language is and how language performs, that any coherent account of the capacity of human speech to communicate meaning and feeling is, in the final analysis, underwritten by the assumption of God's presence.'[12]

What all these writers are acknowledging is that only the existence of one true God makes coherent, real, objective meaning possible. The Christian apologist Cornelius Van Til

---

11 To 'halt meaning' is to acknowledge that meaning is fixed rather than endlessly fluid. It means to halt the endless shifting of meaning characteristic of the so-called 'post-modern' worldview.

12 George Steiner, *Real Presences* (Chicago: University of Chicago Press, 1989), p. 3

has pointed out that when unbelievers reason and speak, and they expect us to understand them, they are actually using 'borrowed capital'[13]; because their very reasoning and speaking is evidence of God, and not only of God, but of the Mediator between men and God, the man Christ Jesus. The Bible is Christ's book because it is the book in which the Father God (the source of all meaning) is made known to human beings.[14] Graeme Goldsworthy rightly concludes that we must make 'the conscious decision to work at the relationships of all parts of the Bible to the gospel' (that is, the gospel of Christ).[15]

The plain meaning of a text

It is important to hold on to this truth: that the Bible has an objective and stable meaning, because there is a true God, and because Jesus Christ is the Mediator between God and people. But we need to clarify what is intended by saying this. We ought to distinguish the *meaning* of the Bible from its *effects* on us. When someone says, 'this passage means something to me', what they are saying, strictly speaking, is that 'this passage – with its fixed objective meaning – is at the moment having this *effect* on me; I am grasping that the *implications* of this text for me are ...' There is, therefore, a difference between two people saying that a text has two objectively different meanings, and saying that a text with one meaning has more than one implication. It may imply certain particular responses for one person in their particular circumstances, and different responses (in detail and specifics) for another person in their very different circumstances.

---

13 Quoted in Graeme Goldsworthy, *Gospel-centred Hermeneutics* (Nottingham: IVP/Apollos, 2006), p. 206

14 Goldsworthy speaks of, 'the soteriological *and hermeneutical* priority of the gospel of Christ' and points out that our rebellious thinking will always conspire 'to lead us ... towards a Christless interpretation' and that is why we see so often 'the eclipse of Christ in hermeneutics'. Graeme Goldsworthy, *Gospel-centred Hermeneutics* (Nottingham: IVP/Apollos, 2006), p. 47f, 72

15 Graeme Goldsworthy, *Gospel-centred Hermeneutics* (Nottingham: IVP/Apollos, 2006), p. 62

Let us explore this briefly. When I speak of 'the meaning' of a text, I mean more than just what the words are and in what order they appear. A text does consist of words in a particular order and with particular forms (for example, singular or plural). But that does not get us very far. Stopping there is a bit like the kind of translation you get from a rather primitive translation programme, that just tells you what each word means in turn, or software that translates a Bible text word for word from the Greek or Hebrew. It will tell you about the text, but it will not tell you what the text is about. By 'meaning' I am speaking not just of 'what somebody said', but rather of 'what somebody meant by what they said'. The meaning is not just the words; it is what the speaker or writer is doing with the words. Is he or she making a promise, for example, or expressing surprise, or giving a command?[16]

So, for example, if a speaker says the words, 'Jesus fed 5,000 people' he or she could put a variety of meanings into those words. He might mean it as a straight, flat, factual assertion, 'I believe that Jesus did feed 5,000 people.' Alternatively, he might mean, 'Jesus fed 5,000 people?! You can't be serious and ask me to believe anything so absurd!' Or it might be the rhetorical question of a preacher, 'Jesus fed 5,000 people? Yes, of course He did! And He has the same power today!'

Another writer[17] has distinguished 'what the text says' from 'what the text means' using the image of 'thin' and 'thick' description of a text. So a 'thin' description just tells me what the text consists of, which words in which forms in what order. But a 'thick' description tells me what they mean. He gives an illustration of a wink. A 'thin' description of a wink might

---

16   In his seminal book *How to do things with words*, J. L. Austin calls the words themselves the 'locution' and the meaning of the words the 'illocution'. He goes on to speak of the effect of the words on the hearer as the "perlocution" (which will be subject of our chapter 7 and the conclusion). By 'the meaning of a text' I mean what Austin calls the locution plus the illocution.

17   Gilbert Ryle, in Vanhoozer, *Is There A Meaning In This Text?* (Leicester: Apollos, 1998), p. 285

say it is 'a rapid contraction of his right eyelid'. But a 'thick' description would tell you, for example, that it was a flirtatious wink across a crowded room, or a mocking imitation of another boy's wink in the playground, or whatever. One tells you what it is, the other what it means.

When we speak of the meaning of a Bible text we are speaking of 'thick' description. As N.T. Wright has helpfully pointed out, when the Reformers insisted that we should read the Bible according to its 'literal' meaning, they meant by this the meaning that the Bible authors meant. So, as he puts it, the 'literal' meaning is the 'literary' meaning.[18] So, for example, if a Christian is asked, 'Do you believe Genesis 1 literally?' we ought to say 'Yes. Yes, I believe it means what the author meant, and that meaning is true.' The question then is, what did the author mean? That, of course, is where the debates start.

Sometimes this 'literal' sense is called 'the plain sense'. So the scholar G.B. Caird writes, 'Whenever Christians have attempted to give to the scriptures a sense other than *the plain sense* intended by those who wrote them, Christianity has been in danger of running out into the sands of Gnosticism.'[19]

For the moment, let us leave to one side what effect, if any, the words have upon the hearers or readers. We shall come back to that in chapter 7 and the conclusion. A text means something, and I understand it if I grasp what it means, whether or not I respond the way the writer or speaker wants me to.

The stability of meaning

There is an idea around that meaning does not reside in the text but in the interaction of the text with the reader. Sometimes this uses the language of horizons. A horizon expresses both a standpoint (from which I look) and a limit to how far I can see. A horizon involves a standpoint and limitations. So I most

18   N. T. Wright, *The Last Word: Beyond the Bible Wars to a New Understanding of the Authority of Scripture* (San Francisco: HarperCollins, 2005), p. 73f

19   Kevin J. Vanhoozer, *Is there a meaning in this text?* (Leicester: IVP/Apollos, 1998), p. 303, my italics

certainly have a horizon. I 'stand' somewhere, and I cannot see very far. I come to a text with a preunderstanding, with prejudices, with my personal history and all that this has made me.

But, it is said, a text also has a horizon. Whoever wrote the text had a standpoint and limitations. When I read a text, my horizon intersects with the horizon of the text. And the meaning, it is suggested, comes from the way our two horizons fuse. Meaning is a co-creation of text and reader. Interpretation is a dialogue: I expose myself to the horizon of the text, but I also expose the text to my horizon and – to some extent – fuse its horizon with mine.

Or, to put it another way, a text is like a musical score that I am invited to perform, or like stars in the sky so that I am invited to 'join the dots' to make from them the constellations I think will be suitable[20]. The text is there; but different readers may legitimately read it different ways, and some or even all their readings may be valid.

This is a very dangerous idea, for it cuts the link between the text and its author. Robert Morgan, of Oxford University, has put it like this, 'Texts, like dead men, have no rights, no aims, no interests. They can be used in whatever way readers or interpreters choose.' [21] Well, they can, but not without doing violence to the author.

This matters more than ever when considering Scripture. For Scripture is not like a dead man. It is the living word of the divine Author. And there is no way my horizon can modify or expand His horizon, which is infinite. What He has communicated, He has communicated. Meaning is not a co-creation between us and Him; it is His creation and gift to us.

---

20   Ricoeur and Iser quoted in Kevin J. Vanhoozer, *Is there a meaning in this text?* (Leicester: IVP/Apollos, 1998), p. 108

21   Robert Morgan, with John Barton, *Biblical Interpretation* (Oxford: Oxford University Press, 1988), p. 7

The Spirit and understanding the Bible

My job is not to fuse His horizon with mine, but rather to align my horizon with His.

A text has a meaning. It may have different *effects* on different hearers or readers, but it has a fixed and stable meaning. It means something[22]. A reader must decide how to respond, but the reader cannot alter the meaning. So when we are doing our Bible interpretation, we are not in a playground having fun making it mean what we want it to mean, and caring little if others make it mean something else. We are engaged in the earnest life-and-death business of discerning the meaning that is there, by which the Father is made known.

THE COMPLETENESS OF THE BIBLE AS TESTIMONY TO CHRIST

It is all very well to claim that a text has an objective meaning. But the critical question we need to ask for understanding a text is, what is its context? We understand a text from its context. Context is the key. To take one example, if I say 'The future is bright, the future is Orange' (an advertising slogan for a mobile network some years ago), the context will probably tell you that I am promoting a mobile phone company. But if I wrote something like that as graffiti on a wall in Belfast, the context might suggest another meaning, for the word 'Orange' has all sorts of other connotations in Northern Ireland. If someone says of a woman, 'She's hot', only the context will determine whether this is a comment about her being angry, or pretty or having an above-normal body temperature. Or, to take an example of Graeme Goldsworthy, the number 60 inside a red circle on a sign by the roadside, may mean 60mph or 60kph, and only the context (i.e. which country we are in) will tell us.

Now let's unpack this in three ways. Here are three ways in which context enables functional literacy so that communication is possible.

---

22 This meaning may include subtleties like irony, ambiguity, and a range of allusion and connotation (especially in poetry) as well as simple denotation. I am not suggesting that meaning is flat and two-dimensional.

1. Language

The most significant overall context for any text is the language in which it is spoken. If I see the letters 'p-a-i-n' I need to know whether it is in French or English. Vanhoozer calls language a city inhabited by writers and readers, speakers and hearers.[23] It is a city with conventions which govern how meaning is communicated. Language is rule-governed behaviour. Words behave differently in different contexts (for example 'love' in a tennis match or 'love' over a candlelit dinner). We need to learn communicative competence, both in speaking/writing and in hearing/reading.

And so the first thing I need to be biblically literate is the Bible languages, Hebrew, Aramaic and Greek, or (for most of us) to lean on trustworthy people who translate the Bible into a language I do understand. We thank God for them. Because although a translation is approximate, and punctuation and paragraphing are not part of Scripture as originally given, nevertheless it does give *adequate* access to the Word of God.

That was, of course, the first step in challenging the interpretive tyranny of the Roman Church at the Reformation. We rejoice in Tyndale's famous saying, when confronted by a smug cleric, "Ere long, if my life be spared, I will cause the boy who driveth the plough to know more of the Bible than you do, Sir'. He challenged the interpretive tyranny of a priestly elite by putting the Bible into the hands of the whole people of God in their own language.

2. Genre

Second, within language, the most important context for the reading of a text is what we call 'genre' (from Latin *genus* = kind). Every piece of writing is a *kind* of something. We need to recognise it as comedy or tragedy, romance, irony, poetry, history, fantasy, and so on. We read *The Lord of the Rings* in one way, the proceedings of Parliament (*Hansard*) in another.

---

23   Kevin J. Vanhoozer, *Is there a meaning in this text?* (Leicester: IVP/Apollos, 1998), pp. 202-7

The Spirit and understanding the Bible

A genre is as it were a suburb of the city of language. And one of the tasks of becoming a competent communicator is to get to know more and more of the suburbs. So M. Bakhtin writes that, 'Many people who have an excellent command of a language often feel quite helpless in certain spheres of communication precisely because they do not have a practical command of the generic forms used in the given spheres'.[24]

In order for communication to be successful both speaker and listeners, or writer and readers, need – as it were – to inhabit the same suburb, to live in a shared world. It is genre that makes this possible. The writer needs to be competent in the genre he writes, and the reader needs to be competent in recognising and reading that genre. Vanhoozer also says that genres are like different kinds of maps. Just as different kinds of map will show different features of a region – perhaps roads, or geological formations, or political boundaries – and each is useful for a different purpose, so different genres are suited to different forms of communication. Different Bible genres communicate different facets of Bible truth.

And, of course, within a genre there are all sorts of smaller linguistic features, such as idioms. Communicative competence is a skill to be learnt. Functional illiteracy surfaces again and again. I remember once mentioning the new heavens and new earth in a sermon. At the end an anxious questioner came up to me to ask, 'But which will we live in, the new heavens or the new earth?' But 'the new heavens and new earth' refers not to two separate realities (the new heavens and – separately – the new earth) but to one united reality.

So biblical literacy needs first a knowledge of, or accurate translation of, the Bible languages; and second a grasp of the Bible genres. If translators are the servants of the church in doing the first, then preachers and teachers are servants of the church in equipping Christians with linguistic competence for the second.

---

24   Ibid., p. 336 n. 372

3. Canon

These first two points, language and genre, are true for any text. But there is another aspect to the context of Scripture. Scripture is a closed book, that is a book with bookends, a book that is not to be added to nor subtracted from. It is the complete revelation of the Father in Jesus Christ.

There is a big difference between a book and a text. A book is a closed totality. It is bound together. It has front and back covers. It is to be read as a meaningful whole. The meaning of any part is to be found in its relation to the whole. But a text is much more fluid. We see it all the time in the fluidity of e-mails or Word documents. A text can so easily be edited, shortened, or expanded, and therefore its meaning changed. Some years ago a journalist wrote in *The Times*, 'Some months ago I made a disobliging remark about a forthcoming novel by Lance Price, Tony Blair's former spin doctor. I wrote: "Perhaps Mr Price's effort will be the corking political novel that Blair's Britain so badly needs, but somehow I am doubtful." Mr Price's book came out this month, and on the front is this ringing endorsement: "The corking political novel that Blair's Britain so badly needs." My words have been taken, spun, and their meaning turned by 180°.'[25]

That is an extreme example. But the moment I have control over the extent of a text, the moment I have it, as it were, on my laptop in electronic form, I can change its meaning. Everyone who has written for a journal knows that. I wrote an article some while ago, and the journal added a sentence near the start which completely altered the meaning. They were courteous enough to show it to me first, and I removed it.

The fact that Christian Scripture is a canon is very important. Vanhoozer contrasts this with the rabbis' approach to the Law of Moses, in which texts lead to commentaries, and the commentaries themselves are then incorporated into the larger body of authoritative text, and so on without limit. So,

---

25   Ben Macintyre reported in *The Week* 19.11.05

for the rabbis, commentary does not aim at a determinative reading, but is part of an ongoing and limitless process, open for ever. And therefore its meaning can never be stable. Any open text, a fluid text, becomes a kind of adventure playground of interpretation.

But the Bible itself claims to be a closed text, a canon, a coherent and completed work[26]. And therefore the meaning of any part is to be understood from the context of the whole. As the Westminster Confession puts it, 'The infallible rule of interpretation of Scripture is Scripture itself'. Article XX of the 39 Articles of the Church of England includes the words, '…it is not lawful for the church … so (to) expound one place of Scripture, that it be repugnant to another.' That is, the text of Scripture as a whole contains those contexts that control the literal sense, the plain sense (plain, that is, to those who know Scripture as a whole). This is the place of biblical theology in interpretation.

The closed canon of Scripture sheds light on the question of seeing a deeper meaning (the so-called *Sensus Plenior*, or fuller meaning) in texts, especially Old Testament texts, that is to say, a meaning that goes beyond any meaning that the original author consciously understood. What we are doing when we see this fuller meaning is not superimposing an alien meaning that is inconsistent with what they originally thought it meant. Instead, we are seeing more of the fullness of the meaning they discerned only in part. So, for example, when we read in the Psalms of the sufferings of a righteous believer who entrusts himself to God for vindication, we understand that those texts spoke more fully than their authors knew, in foreshadowing the sufferings and subsequent glory of Jesus Christ.

There is here an analogy with events in history. An event in human history can only be provisionally understood within

---

26 This is appropriately signalled not just for Revelation, but for the whole canon, in Revelation 22:18,19. And it is implied by texts such as Hebrews 1:1-3 and 1 John 1:1-4, and the many ways in which the New Testament claims that Christ is the final fulfilment of Old Testament promise.

history. When 9/11 happened, it was impossible at the time to assess the long-term significance of this terrible event. As time goes on, it becomes easier to form a judgement with some historical perspective (which is why historians generally prefer to write history with some distance between them and the events they describe and analyse). But it is only when history is completed that the full significance of that event will be seen.

In the same way, all sorts of things were said in the Old Testament that indicated a meaning that was necessarily somewhat indefinite, even hazy. Peter speaks of the prophets who 'searched intently and with the greatest care, trying to find out the time and circumstances to which the Spirit of Christ in them was pointing when he predicted the sufferings of Christ and the glories that would follow' (1 Pet. 1:10, 11). It was only as the closed canon of Scripture came to completion after Christ that the full significance of a particular text can be understood. From the viewpoint of the completed canon we can see the full meaning. That meaning does not contradict the original conscious authorial intention of, say, Isaiah. But it fills it out. This fuller sense is the literal sense taken at the level of its 'thickest' description. It is what it fully meant.[27]

We need, therefore, to learn to view Scripture as a whole and to read individual texts within Scripture not on their own, but as parts of Scripture as a whole. Fragmentary reading is like viewing an Impressionist painting from too close up. Only when we step back do we see, for example, Rouen Cathedral at sunrise. The interpretive principle of the canon is *integration* rather than fragmentation. Scripture is not just the word of Christ; it is the finished word of Christ. Without that finish, we are still with the rabbis, commentary upon commentary without limit.

---

27 Speaking of this kind of typological reading, Hans Frei writes that, 'Far from being in conflict with the literal sense ... typology was a natural extension of literal interpretation. It was *literalism at the level of the whole biblical story* ...' Hans Frei, *The Eclipse of Biblical Narrative. A Study in Eighteenth and Nineteenth Century Hermeneutics* (New Haven: Yale University Press, 1974), p. 2 my italics.

The Spirit and understanding the Bible

This principle of a closed canon is so important for contemporary understanding and application of the Bible that I am going to spend some time exploring how it is understood – in my view misunderstood – by two contemporary writers, one scholarly, the other popular.

I. Howard Marshall: going 'Beyond the Bible'

I. Howard Marshall is one of the most distinguished evangelical biblical scholars of the mid to late-twentieth century. In 2004 he published *Beyond the Bible: moving from Scripture to Theology*, based on lectures given at an American college, and including printed responses from Kevin Vanhoozer and Stanley Porter. Marshall's aim was 'to open up the question of how we get from the Bible to Christian doctrine and practice in the contemporary world'.[28] It is an important question, but I have deep misgivings about the kind of answers Marshall suggests.

I want to focus on one part of that answer. Marshall cites with approval the idea of W. J. Webb that within the Bible we have a 'redemptive trajectory' which will lead us to seek 'a fuller redemption than was envisaged in the New Testament'.[29] This theory builds on the acknowledged fact that there is a significant change from the Old Covenant/Testament to the New. But it goes further and claims that such a movement should happen, not just once from the Old Testament to the New, but again and again – not a one-off 'step' but a 'trajectory'. And notice that word 'envisaged'. Webb is not just saying that there is more redeeming to be done. That is clearly true, and until we finally experience 'the redemption of our bodies' (Rom. 8:23) we shall be longing for more and fuller redemption. But Webb is suggesting that we should look for a fuller redemption than the New Testament writers had in their minds or expressed in their writings. That is to say, we should go beyond the Bible. We

---

28   I. Howard Marshall, *Beyond the Bible: moving from Scripture to Theology* (Grand Rapids, Michigan: Baker, 2004), p. 31

29   Ibid., p. 38

should expect further truth that will develop and even correct what we find in the New Testament.

In line with this idea, Marshall raises the question of whether the Bible books included in the canon, 'constitute a conclusion to doctrinal and ethical development or whether they offer a pattern that the church can continue to follow'.[30] In his lectures, Marshall seems to favour the latter, with 'the possibility of new revelations' through a prophet, with the developments from the Old to the New Covenant being continued by 'further developments', and with these further developments being guided by 'a mind nurtured on the gospel', that is to say by 'a combination of the apostolic deposit and Spirit-given insight'.[31]

Marshall's language is carefully nuanced, but it makes me uneasy. We get one indication of where it might lead when Marshall discusses our distaste for the terrible judgements visited on some of the characters in Jesus' parables. 'Worst of all' these examples, he suggests, 'is the command of the king who has his enemies brought into his presence and killed before his very eyes (Luke 19:27).' We find this and other such judgements 'unacceptable' today and 'It is incredible that God should so act.' We must conclude, suggests Marshall, that 'we can no longer think of God in that way, even if this is imagery used by Jesus. Our basis lies in a mind nurtured by the Spirit, the mind of Christ…'[32]. So it seems that there may be a tension between 'the Spirit' and the written word of the New Testament. Somehow the Spirit, giving us 'the mind of Christ' can contradict the imagery used by Christ according to the Gospels.

As Vanhoozer points out, this idea of 'a mind nurtured on the gospel' leaves us with a terrible uncertainty. For example, when expounding his idea of a 'redemptive trajectory', Webb thinks it leads to an egalitarian view of men and women (in

---

30   Ibid., p. 54

31   Ibid., pp. 61, 62, 70, 71

32   Ibid., p. 66f

contradiction of the complementarian view taught, for example, in Ephesians 5) but not to the approval of same-sex intimacy. But other writers 'appeal to the very same logic of redemptive trajectory in order to legitimate same-sex relations'[33].

What in practice this approach means is that the written word is trumped by the authority of 'the Spirit', where what is called 'the Spirit' is actually more like the spirit of the age. This ends with a practical evacuation of authority from the revelation of the Father in Christ attested by Scripture. We shall explore in chapters 6–7 and the conclusion what a more biblical and stable doctrine of the ministry of the Spirit would be for us today.

Rob Bell: doctrine as flexible springs on a trampoline

My popular example is the American pastor Rob Bell (mentioned earlier, p. 64). In the Introduction to his book *Velvet Elvis,* Bell tells us about a painting he has of Elvis Presley. It would be absurd, he suggests, if the painter had suggested that this was the final and definitive painting of Elvis. In the same way, just as art has to 'keep going…exploring, keep arranging, keep shaping and forming and bringing in new perspectives' so with Christianity. We are not just to make 'cosmetic, superficial changes' but also to change 'theology: the beliefs about God, Jesus, the Bible, salvation and the future.' Doctrines are like the springs of his family trampoline. They are flexible. And just as the springs of the trampoline are means to the end of enjoying the jumping, so Christian doctrines are just the means to the end of experiencing the Christian life, living the way of Jesus. When we say that doctrines are fixed, like bricks in a rigid wall, we replace Christianity with what he disparagingly calls, 'brickianity'.[34]

---

33 Response essay in I. Howard Marshall, *Beyond the Bible: moving from Scripture to Theology* (Grand Rapids, Michigan: Baker, 2004), p. 90. Vanhoozer names Luke Johnson and Stephen Fowl as those who argue that the redemptive trajectory should include affirming same-sex intimacy

34 Rob Bell, *Velvet Elvis* (Grand Rapids, Michigan: Zondervan, 2005), pp. 10-13, 22-8

Christianity is not about knowing anything definitely, for 'if we do definitively put God into words, we have at that moment made God something God is not.' Rather, we are to learn to live with mystery (quoting the great theologian Sean Penn, 'The mystery *is* the truth'). 'The very nature of orthodox Christian faith is that we never come to the end. It begs for more. More discussion, more inquiry, more debate, more questions. It's not so much that the Christian faith *has* a lot of paradoxes. It's that it *is* a lot of paradoxes. And we cannot resolve a paradox. We have to let it be what it is.'[35] How very different this is from real Christianity in which Jesus Christ made the Father known. If we listen to Bell, we will think that Jesus made the unknown Father even more unknown!

It may seem incongruous to mention one distinguished scholar (I. Howard Marshall) alongside one popular writer but, as David Wells has perceptively noted, 'A line connects Marshall … to … Bell. It is that the authority of God functions separately from the written Scriptures'.[36]

A WORD OF CAUTION: WE SHOULD RESPECT CHRISTIAN TRADITION

At this point I feel I need to add a cautionary word. In his lucid and outstandingly helpful book *Words of Life*, Timothy Ward gives a healthy and necessary corrective against individualistic interpretations of the Bible.[37] We need to recognise that interpreting and understanding the Bible is not done as a solo exercise by individual believers. We seek to sit under the Bible together. And we do so together not only with our contemporary Christians all over the world, but also with the great line of believers all down the ages. We are not the first post-apostolic generation to believe the Bible. In the first five or so centuries of the church, those who taught the Bible were guided by the

---

35 Ibid., pp. 32-4

36 David F. Wells, *The Courage to be Protestant* (Nottingham: IVP, 2008), p. 87

37 Timothy Ward, *Words of Life* (Nottingham: IVP, 2009), pp. 143-53

The Spirit and understanding the Bible

understanding that there are in the Bible a number of central gospel principles. The second-century church leader Tertullian gave these the name, 'the rule of faith'. These principles acted as a helpful guide to keep the detail of Bible interpretation in line with the central themes of the Bible as whole. It acted as a safeguard against idiosyncratic or unorthodox interpretations of particular passages, through which error could be introduced to the church.

Sadly, the late medieval Western church (which looked to the Pope in Rome for a lead) moved away from this to an understanding in which there were two parallel (and to some extent independent) sources of authority: Scripture and also now the traditional teaching of the church (the church's *magisterium*), or the Pope speaking *ex cathedra*, out of his official teaching chair or throne (the *cathedra*), in his official capacity. Correcting this error, and bringing the church back to its early church roots, the Reformers said we must go back to one source of authority, and coined their famous cry 'Sola Scriptura!' (Scripture Alone!). There must be no second or supplementary source of teaching authority in the church. But – and this is the important point – in their Bible teaching, the mainline Reformers (such as Martin Luther, Ulrich Zwingli and John Calvin) had a very great respect for the Bible commentators and preachers of the previous generations, and especially for those of the first five or so centuries. Although they did not regard them as having ultimate authority, nevertheless they valued the great central traditions of interpretation. They particularly esteemed the great Creeds of the early centuries, and expounded the Bible in line with those central guiding principles.

There was, however, a minority radical movement in the Reformation who did not share this respect for tradition. Their cry, which one modern writer had dubbed 'Solo Scriptura' (Scripture interpreted all on my own!) rather than 'Sola Scriptura', was that the individual, guided and led by the Spirit, could interpret the Scripture without the help and guidance of other Christians in the past. It was a kind of 'hotline to God' model, and it has had its heirs and successors in every generation of the church. Timothy Ward draws attention to the dangers with this kind of shallow and individualistic model, and rightly suggests that some contemporary evangelicalism is marked more by 'Solo Scriptura' than by 'Sola Scriptura'.

When this happens, unrealistic claims are made about how 'the spirit' (but is it Spirit or spirit?) can lead the individual to understand the Bible in isolation. When such people speak of 'the spirit' we must ask which spirit is guiding them. There is a healthy place for respecting and taking account of how Christians have understood apostolic truth down the generations. Their understandings cannot be our authority, which is Scripture alone. But if we think the Bible means something that nobody else has thought, it is just possible we are wrong! Against Christians who prefer the individual hotline approach, Charles Spurgeon commented that, 'It seems odd, that certain men who talk so much of what the Holy Spirit reveals to themselves, should think so little of what he had revealed to others…' This leads, as Spurgeon observed, to erratic thinking, 'wild interpretations and outrageous inferences'[38].

THE EXTERNAL CLARITY OF THE BIBLE AS TESTIMONY TO CHRIST

It is possible to understand the Bible.[39] Luther called this truth, the 'clarity of Scripture' (*claritas Scripturae*). It was the chief weapon for combating hermeneutical tyranny at the time of the Reformation. So, in his great work *The Bondage of the Will*, written in debate against Erasmus, Luther engages with the claim of Erasmus that some Christian doctrines are obscure. Luther agrees that 'many *passages* in the Scriptures are obscure and

---

38   quoted in Iain Murray, *The Old Evangelicalism* (Edinburgh: Banner of Truth, 2005), pp. xii and xiii

39   The most helpful – and appropriately lucid – treatment of the clarity of Scripture is Mark D. Thompson, *A Clear and Present Word* (New Studies in Biblical Theology. Nottingham: IVP/Apollos, 2006)

hard to elucidate' but this is only because of 'our own linguistic and grammatical ignorance'. But – and this is Luther's main argument – since the coming of Christ the *contents* of Scripture have become very plain. 'Take Christ from the Scriptures – and what more will you find in them?' Luther understood that the unity and clarity of Scripture is that they are the revelation of God the Father in Christ. Besides, 'If words are obscure in one place, they are clear in another'. So it doesn't matter that there are some obscure texts. 'Who will maintain that the town fountain does not stand in the light because the people down some alley cannot see it, while everyone in the square can see it?' So if I find myself in an obscure text ('down some alley') all I have to do to see the truth clearly is move into a clearer text (the town square)[40].

The clarity of Scripture does not mean that we can know for certain the answers to all our questions about the interpretation of Scripture. Nor does it give *carte blanche* to every idiosyncratic individual to interpret how they like (despite the impression we may give to our Roman Catholic friends). There are interpretations that deserve to be put in what one writer called 'the exegetical curiosity cabinet'. Rather, it means that an honest interpreter can grasp enough to know how we ought to respond, and will be held responsible for responding as we ought. It is not so much about the obviousness of Scripture as about its efficacy.

Luther distinguished helpfully between what he called the 'external clarity' of Scripture and its 'internal clarity'.

> 'In a word: The perspicuity (*claritas*) of Scripture is twofold…
> The first is external, and relates to the ministry of the Word; the second concerns the knowledge of the heart. If you speak of *internal* perspicuity, the truth is that nobody who has not the Spirit of God sees a jot of what is in the Scriptures. All men have their hearts darkened, so that, even

---

40   Martin Luther, *The Bondage of the Will* (translated J. I. Packer and O. R. Johnston, London: James Clarke, 1957), p. 71f

when they can discuss and quote all that is in Scripture, they do not understand or really know any of it... The Spirit is needed for the understanding of all Scripture and every part of Scripture. If, on the other hand, you speak of *external* perspicuity, the position is that nothing whatsoever is left obscure or ambiguous, but all that is in the Scripture is through the Word brought forth into the clearest light and proclaimed to the whole world'[41].

By its external clarity he meant pretty much what I mean by grasping the meaning. A well-intentioned interpreter competent with the language and literature (i.e. with the various genres) can adequately grasp the literal meaning. By its internal clarity he meant the work of the Spirit in the believing reader. This is more to do with our response, and is the subject of chapter 7 and the conclusion.

CONCLUSION

In this chapter I hope our confidence has been boosted that we can understand and interpret the Bible. That is to say, we can understand sufficiently what it meant and means, and we can deduce from this how we ought to respond to it today. And therefore we can have the Father God made known to us through it. This is the goal of interpreting the Bible. We cannot avoid doing interpretation, but our aim must always be that it leads us to walk in fellowship with the Father and the Son. We must remember that it is the book of Christ; He is its Subject and He is its Interpreter. He is the mediator of meaning. It is by His ministry that the Father is made known. So we read the whole Bible as centred and focused on the great revelation of the Father in Christ. What is more, it is the closed testimony to the complete revelation of the Father in Christ. The context for Bible meanings is the whole Bible. An honest and competent reader who has access to a reliable translation and develops a good knowledge of the whole Bible, can read it

---

41   Ibid., p. 73f

and understand it, entirely adequately, though never of course completely.

STUDY AND DISCUSSION QUESTIONS

1. What is the proper goal of Bible interpretation? How will this affect the spirit in which you read and study the Bible, both on your own and with others?

2. What are the dangers and difficulties in discovering God through a discussion based on questions the Bible asks rather than using the answers the Bible gives?

3. The Bible is the book of Christ. How does this affect the way we read any particular part of it?

4. What do we mean when we speak of 'the plain meaning' of a text in the Bible? How ought we to distinguish this from its effects on a particular person?

5. Why is context so important for understanding any text? How does the big context of the whole canon of Scripture affect how we understand the Bible?

6. How ought we to view the traditions of interpreting the Bible in the history of the church? Why?

6

The Spirit and other spirits

The main focus of chapters 1, 3, 4 and 5 has been on the unique, sufficient and complete revelation of the Father through Jesus Christ, and how that revelation is reliably attested to us by the whole Bible. Before we come to our final and positive focus on the authentic ministry of the Spirit of God, we need a cautionary chapter of warning.

Let us start by going back to a surprising and thought-provoking saying of Jesus. In the context of a sobering section of text in which Jesus is speaking of the hatred that His disciples must expect from a hostile world (John 15:18–16:4), Jesus says this:

> 'When the Counsellor comes, whom I will send to you from the Father, the Spirit of truth who goes out from the Father, he will testify about me. And you also must testify, for you have been with me from the beginning.' (John 15:26, 27)

Jesus speaks here of two witnesses. There is the witness or testimony of the Holy Spirit to Jesus. And there is the witness of the apostles to Jesus. Why both? Why is it not enough that

God the Holy Spirit should bear witness to God the Son? After all, the Spirit is God. Is the testimony of God insufficient? Why must the apostles bear witness in addition to His testimony? It seems a bit like saying to me (as a rather modest amateur tennis player), 'The Wimbledon champion needs a bit of help. Would you go on court to play beside him, and you can help him win?' It would be nonsense. I might as well sit by the court sipping Robinson's Lemon Barley Water for all the good I could do. If God the Holy Spirit is going to bear witness to Jesus, why do the apostles need to bother?

It makes no sense unless their testimony and the Spirit's testimony are of different kinds. Unless He is not supplementing their incompleteness with more of the same (in which case He might as well take over the whole job, for He would do it better), but rather complementing their testimony with a different kind of witness. And this is exactly what He does, as we shall explore in chapter 7.

Christianity is neither bare history nor fluid mysticism[1]. It is not bare history, as we might say disparagingly of someone who is past his best, 'Oh, he's history'. And it is not fluid mysticism, a religion understood and perceived by subjective experience. But like a hiker walking along a high ridge, we are always in danger of falling off to the left or to the right, into bare history with no living experience or experience with no anchor in truth. The key to staying on the ridge, staying Christian, is to be clear on the different and complementary natures of these two testimonies, and to see why both are needed. In this chapter we are going to focus on the apostles' testimony to Jesus, and in chapter 7 on the witness of the Spirit to Jesus.

The testimony of the apostles to the complete revelation of the Father in the earthly ministry of Jesus, from His anointing with the Spirit at His baptism until His Ascension, is essential

---

1 The Oxford English Dictionary lists eight distinct uses of the word "mysticism". I endeavour to use it consistently in the sense of a purely subjective experience, and therefore an experience not testable by objective criteria and not anchored to objective truth.

to anchor and root Christianity in history and objective truth. Without this anchor, Christianity metamorphoses into a subjective mystical experience with a vaguely Christian flavour. The transition from experience anchored in history into fluid mystical experience is not always easy to spot. But it marks a paradigm shift and it signals the abandonment of truth.

THE JESUS OF HISTORY AND THE CHRIST OF FAITH

The old debate between the so-called 'Jesus of history' and the 'Christ of faith' parallels our study of word and Spirit in some ways. The expression, 'The so-called historical Jesus and the historic biblical Christ'[2] was coined by the German theologian Martin Kähler in 1892 to distinguish between two ways of approaching Jesus. On the one hand there was the – in his view flawed and futile – search for the historical Jesus, the subject of the famous so-called 'Quest for the historical Jesus' that characterised much of nineteenth-century liberal Protestantism. On the other hand, said Kähler, there is the authentic (in his terms, 'historic' using a different German word) Christ of biblical faith. The expressions 'the Jesus of history' and 'the Christ of faith' have since come to be used by those who suggest that we may make a distinction and separation between Jesus as He actually was in history and the Christ we proclaim, worship and trust today.

When and if we treat Christianity as purely a matter of history we focus on 'the Jesus of history'. The trouble is that He then becomes just a dead letter, a character in a museum. When and if we treat Christianity as a matter only of 'the Christ of faith', we lapse either into traditionalism (which is a common characteristic of much Roman Catholicism), where we trust the Christ who has been handed down to us by the church, or into mysticism, where we trust the Christ of our own subjective experience. The 'Christ of faith' becomes either an individual

---

2   *The So-Called Historical Jesus and the Historic Biblical Christ*, trans. C. E. Braaten (Philadelphia: Fortress, 1964), from the 1896 German edition

creation of the imagination of my own heart (masquerading as 'spiritual') or a collective assertion of institutional tradition. Any attempt or tendency to divorce the two leads away from orthodox Christianity.

It is interesting to see how this old debate has been popularised recently by the anti-Christian children's writer Philip Pullman in his book, *The good man Jesus and the scoundrel Christ*[3]. Pullman uses the mischievous narrative fancy of there being two brothers (one called Jesus, the other called Christ). Onto one (Jesus) he projects the bits of the Jesus story he likes. Onto the other (Christ) he projects the bits he doesn't like. He suggests that the one is history and the other is a later creation of the Church. This is deeply misleading. One of the earliest corrections of error comes in John's first letter, where he needs to insist that 'Jesus Christ has come in the flesh' that is to say the man Jesus is the Christ, the anointed one or Messiah of God, come in the flesh (1 John 4:2). Any teaching that separates the man Jesus from the Christ is not Christianity. There is no 'ugly ditch... between the Jesus of history and the Christ of faith' (in Lessing's infamous phrase).

THE SIGNIFICANCE OF THE BODILY INCARNATION OF CHRIST

The reason the apostles need to bear witness is that the bodily incarnation of Christ is the revelation of the invisible Father. This is why the apostolic testimony extends only to the point where Jesus is taken up from them in the Ascension and not beyond (Acts 1:21, 22). While indeed they (and we) have ongoing spiritual experience of Jesus (e.g. Eph. 3:17-19), their *testimony* is to the historical and physical appearing of Jesus.

The Father was not made known through a spiritual (in the sense of non-bodily) experience; He was revealed by the bodily presence of Jesus Christ. We shall see in chapter 7 that the Spirit does not make the Father known by a purely spiritual

---

3   Philip Pullman, *The good man Jesus and the scoundrel Christ* (London: Canongate, 2010)

(non-bodily) experience, but by bringing home to the heart, mind and will the testimony given to the bodily revelation of the Father. When Christianity metamorphoses into mysticism, a false dualism intrudes, which privileges the 'spiritual' (in the sense of non-bodily) above the bodily experience. This is a false spirituality.

SANCTIFY THEM BY THE TRUTH

The usefulness of the Church to a needy world depends critically on our being anchored firmly in apostolic truth. In His great prayer of John 17, Jesus prays for His apostles that the Father will, 'Sanctify them by the truth; your word is truth' (John 17:17). To 'sanctify' means in this context to set apart for useful ministry and mission. Immediately afterwards Jesus pledges, 'For them I sanctify myself…' (John 17:19). In going to the Cross, Jesus sets Himself apart for His mission. For the apostles, to be set apart and equipped for mission is to be firmly anchored in 'the truth' which is 'your word'. And, as we have repeatedly seen, the Father's word is precisely the word that Jesus has spoken. So the apostles are to be anchored in the words of Jesus, which is exactly what they are, as they launch out on their teaching ministries after Pentecost. It is this 'word' that sets them apart and renders them useful. Without it they would be of no use to the world.

Shortly afterwards, Jesus goes on to say, 'My prayer is not for them alone' (that is, for the apostles alone). 'I pray also for those who will believe in me through their message' (literally, 'through their word') (John 17:20). Men and women do not believe in Jesus through a mystical experience; they believe in Him through the apostolic message. This is exactly what we should expect. For if the Father has been made known by Jesus Christ through His words, and the apostles give authentic testimony to those words, then it is by the apostles' witness and word that the Father is made known today.

The church that holds tenaciously to the Bible will be the church set apart by the Father for the mission of Jesus. The church that sits light to the Bible, that thinks the Bible is just one of a number of parallel sources of revelation, will gradually but surely be absorbed into the surrounding culture. It will be liberal in the next generation, where I use liberal in the theological sense of being conformed to the spirit of the age. This is what happens when a church begins to take the Bible for granted. They do not immediately switch from confident preaching of the Bible to denial of the Bible. First they begin to 'move on' and to take the Bible for granted. 'Of course we believe the Bible,' they say. 'It is just that we find we need something more.' When the Bible is taken for granted in one generation, a church will stop actually teaching and preaching the Bible. And so it will be sidelined in that generation and denied in the next. The church's message gradually blurs; the places where its message jars with the surrounding culture will be the places where the Bible is gradually ignored, so that the terrible doctrines of judgment will be sidelined, for example, and the wrath of God will be replaced by a therapeutic gospel which is there to meet my needs and make me feel better. Before long, that church will cease to be set apart for the mission of Jesus; it will be indistinguishable from the world around.

BLESSED ARE THOSE WHO HAVE NOT SEEN AND YET HAVE BELIEVED

What is the point of the famous story of 'doubting Thomas'? Jesus concludes by saying,

> 'Because you have seen me, you have believed; blessed are those who have not seen and yet have believed.' (John 20:29)

The point of the story is that it signals to us the transition from faith based upon sight to faith based upon testimony[4]. The other

---

4   This is the central emphasis of Dick Lucas and William Philip, *Teaching John* (Ross-shire: Christian Focus/PT Media, 2002)

apostles first saw and then believed. There was nothing wrong with that. Indeed, it is what the apostles were there for, to have that unique eye-witness testimony. If no-one had seen, then none of us could responsibly believe. Jesus does not rebuke Thomas for seeing and then believing. In a way, Thomas is no different from the others: first he saw and then he believed. The only difference is that he 'saw' a week later than the others. Jesus is not so interested in the merits or demerits of Thomas, as in teaching us all that there is about to be a transfer, a change, from those who believe on the basis of sight, to those who believe on the basis of testimony.

The sense of what Jesus says to Thomas would seem to be this: 'Thomas, it is good that you have seen and believed; it would have been even better if you had believed the others when they repeatedly gave you testimony that they had seen the risen Lord.' If Thomas is rebuked, albeit very mildly, it is for not believing the testimony of the others, because Jesus wants us to learn that this is how belief is going to happen from then on. Those who believe on the basis of apostolic testimony will be blessed no less than the apostles were blessed for seeing and then believing. The generations to come are not disadvantaged. It would not have been better to have been there in the Upper Room with the apostles. God will bless every man and woman from then till the end of the world who believes on the basis of the testimony of the apostles.

This is why John goes straight on to conclude,

'Jesus did many other miraculous signs in the presence of his disciples, which are not recorded in this book. But these are written that you may believe that Jesus is the Christ, the Son of God, and that by believing you may have life in his name.' (John 20:30, 31)

In the future, men and women will be blessed by believing the testimony of the eye-witnesses. This is why John takes great care to select and write down signs that Jesus did (and supremely the greatest sign of the resurrection). These, he says, 'are written that you may believe' because from then on to the end of history men and women will believe on the basis of the written apostolic testimony.

It has to be like that, because Christianity is not bare mysticism. The resurrection was an historical event, something that happened to a particular person in a particular place at a particular time. It was an event such that there were particular witnesses, who saw the empty tomb and saw the risen Lord. It was not a mystical phenomenon, such that anybody anywhere at any time might see the risen Lord, perhaps by some technique of meditation or prayer and fasting. No, the physical body of Jesus of Nazareth was raised from the dead never to die again. And some particular people saw Him, heard Him, touched Him, in that real transformed physical body. That happened for just a few weeks, and then He left them. And since He left them, no human being has been with Jesus in that same way. Stephen had a vision of Jesus when he was martyred (Acts 7:56). Paul had a vision of Jesus on the Damascus road (Acts 9), and that vision is clearly unique, for it constituted him to be an apostle ('as one untimely born'…).

But no one else has had a 'Damascus road experience' in that unique sense. No-one has sat with Jesus over a meal the way the apostles did in those days after the resurrection. It is wonderful when, for example, a Muslim has a 'Jesus dream' that is the trigger God uses to bring them to faith. But their experience is qualitatively different from the physical and bodily appearance of Jesus seen by the apostles after the resurrection and by Paul on the Damascus road.

Therefore, it is necessary that the rest of us, if we are to believe, must believe on the basis of the apostles' testimony. And we are blessed if we do. We are not blessed if we believe on any other basis, which is why we need to be warned about false spirits masquerading as the Holy Spirit of Jesus.

WHAT NOT TO BELIEVE: THE DIVINE OBLIGATION TO BE SCEPTICAL

Because Christianity is not mysticism, we are to become skilled in unbelief. Every Christian needs to be a resolute unbeliever as well as being a believer. Writing in his first letter, to Christians in great danger of being deceived, John tells them firmly what not to believe:

> 'Dear friends, do not believe every spirit, but test the spirits to see whether they are from God, because many false prophets have gone out into the world.' (1 John 4:1)

He goes on to tell them how they can 'recognise the Spirit of God' (v. 2) and to conclude, 'This is how we recognise the Spirit of truth and the spirit of falsehood' (v. 6). The criterion he gives them is an objective doctrine, that the man Jesus is the Christ come in the flesh (v. 2). At other times and in other controversies there may be other doctrinal criteria. In Corinth at an earlier date it was the confession that, 'Jesus is Lord' (1 Cor. 12:3). If Christianity had been a form of mysticism, then it would not be appropriate to give an objective doctrinal criterion, for experience would be evidence of authenticity.

Behind every teaching there is a spirit which animates the teacher. John tells us that the proper response to most of them is unbelief. Some people are so 'nice' that we are terribly frightened to be negative about anyone or anything. It goes flat against the spirit of the age to say anyone is wrong. We are told that the great virtue is 'faith', so that 'communities of faith' should get together and work together for the good of mankind. And by 'faith' people mean faith as a subjective human quality, something you or I 'have' or 'don't have'.

But 'faith' as a subjective human attribute is as likely to be a vice as a virtue. It is not good *per se* to be a believer: the question is, 'In what or in whom do we believe? What is the

123

object of our faith?' John says we are to test the spirits to see if they are from God, because most of them aren't.

In Thomas Hardy's novel *Far from the Madding Crowd* he puts these words into the mouth of one character: 'There's this to be said for the Church' (he is speaking of the Church of England), that 'a man can belong to the Church and bide in his cheerful old inn, and never trouble or worry his mind about doctrines at all.' English nice vagueness is a culturally curious variant on Christianity as mysticism.

But John says we must worry our minds about doctrines. We are not to be gullible. If we leave behind the testimony of the apostles we leave behind the Holy Spirit. We will be animated and energised by a spirit. But it will not be the Holy Spirit. There are plenty of spirits out there waiting to don the Holy Spirit's clothes and masquerade as the Holy Spirit.

In 1986 Joyce Huggett published her book *Listening to God* in which she tells of her journey away from traditional evangelical Christianity. She quoted with approval an author saying that 'the whole Bible' is 'simply a written record of ... religious experience... of God speaking to' people, and that the same God speaks in the same ways to people today. But this is to abandon authentic Christianity and embrace a form of mysticism.[5]

While preparing the material in this chapter, I was sent the first issue of a magazine called *The Oxford Theologian*, produced by the Theology Faculty at Oxford University. In his editorial, Professor Diarmaid MacCulloch mentions three articles in the magazine. One is by the Archbishop of Canterbury, one by a former Master of the Dominican Order (about experiencing God in the Eucharist) and one by a former theology undergraduate who has now abandoned her faith altogether to become a clown. He says these three articles 'reflect the glorious cacophony of religious

---

5   Joyce Huggett, *Listening to God* (2nd Edition, London: Hodder & Stoughton, 1996), p. 10

experience, or perhaps better the harmony which comes from contrasting musical voices in a trio of instruments: three aspects of the Divine Comedy which is the exploration of the spiritual in all belief-systems. One expression of this universal religious insight is the Christian affirmation that the Holy Spirit blows where it (sic) wills; there is nothing predictable about where our human explorations of the humanly inexpressible will lead.' Although coming from a very distinguished scholar speaking for the Theology Faculty of a great university, these words have nothing to do with authentic Christianity; they are a thinly veiled affirmation of mysticism with a vaguely Christian flavour. We ought not to believe it.

A CLARIFICATION: HEARING THE BIBLE WITHOUT THE BIBLE

We have seen very forcibly that men and women believe in Jesus through the word of apostolic testimony that we have in Scripture. They do not believe through a mystical experience. But to say this is to invite contradiction from many devout Christians who will tell wonderful stories of men and women coming to faith in Christ initially through precisely such an experience, perhaps a dream or vision. While working on the material for this book, I received a prayer letter from friends working in the Muslim world. It included this extract from an e-mail from an Islamic country: 'I am a new believer in Christ and I met the Lord through a dream.' Such stories could be multiplied. What are we to say to this? Was Jesus wrong to pray for 'those who will believe in me *through their* (the apostles') *message*' (John 17:20)? Ought He also to have prayed for those who would believe in Him through dreams and visions? Does God speak separately from the apostolic testimony in Scripture? What about a so-called 'word of knowledge' or the words of a self-styled contemporary prophet? We will all of us know of people who have claimed revelation from God in some such form, and, so far as we can tell, it has led them to faith in Christ, or strengthened their faith in Christ.

I want to suggest – somewhat tentatively – that the sharp polarisation between the two may be unnecessary. In his book *The Rage against God*, Peter Hitchens tells a moving story of how his conscience was awakened by seeing a fifteenth-century painting of the Last Judgement by Rogier van der Weyden. As he looked at the naked figures going to hell, 'A large catalogue of misdeeds… replayed themselves rapidly in my head. I had absolutely no doubt that I was among the damned, if there were any damned. And what if there were? How did I know there were not? I did not know. I could not know.'[6]

Now in a direct sense he did not get that awakening of conscience from the Bible. There was no Bible open, no-one was reading or preaching to him from the Bible, he was not reading the Bible, there was no Bible text on the painting. But – and this is the point – that painting would not have been painted had it not been for the Bible. So in a secondary sense he got it from the Bible. He got it mediated through a culture that had been soaked in the Bible.

We might say the same about reading *The Pilgrim's Progress*. Spurgeon said of Bunyan that he had studied the Bible, 'till his whole being was saturated with Scripture; and though his writings are charmingly full of poetry, yet he cannot give us his *Pilgrim's Progress* – that sweetest of all prose poems – without continually making us feel and say, "Why, this man is a living Bible!" Prick him anywhere; and you will find that his blood is Bibline, the very essence of the Bible flows from him. He cannot speak without quoting a text, for his soul is full of the Word of God.'[7]

Does God speak through *The Pilgrim's Progress*? Yes, He does, because *Pilgrim's Progress* is soaked in the Bible. Here is a strange (and perhaps a little perverse) analogy with passive or secondary smoking. Suppose you want to get into your lungs the effects of smoking (you can see why this is a perverse illustration). You

---

6   Peter Hitchens, *The Rage against God* (London: Continuum, 2010), p. 75

7   Quoted in John Piper, *Tested by Fire* (Leicester: IVP, 2001), p. 77

could chain-smoke unfiltered cigarettes all day. Alternatively, you could try breathing the air in a room full of smokers. One will get the products of smoking into your lungs directly, the other indirectly. The indirect will likely be less intense, but you will still get it. It will do you harm, even if it does you less harm.

Now reverse that. If you read the Bible or hear it read and preached, you breathe it directly into your mind and heart. If you breathe the air of a culture that has been influenced by the Bible, you may still breathe in something of the Bible's teaching and worldview indirectly. It will be diluted and probably distorted. But some of it will still be there. It may still do you good, but it will likely do you less good. I wonder how many dreams or waking experiences of God that lead people to Jesus are – humanly speaking – the result of breathing the common cultural air of a world deeply influenced by the Bible. I am not at all denying that God may be giving these experiences, merely suggesting that He sometimes generates them through the unconscious faculties of people who live in a world that has been impacted by the apostolic testimony to Christ in the Bible. We must remember that God is able to work through our subconscious and intuitive faculties as much as He is able to work through our conscious and cognitive faculties.

Perhaps some of those dreams are dependent in indirect but important ways on the message of the apostles. But even if a 'Jesus dream' comes to someone who seems not to have had any immersion in Christian culture, we ought to long to 'chain-smoke' the Bible unfiltered. The moment we are happy with secondary Bible smoking, we are en route for no Bible smoking at all. God may kindly do us good through secondary inhalation of His Word. But let's move to unfiltered inhalation as soon as we can. It is very striking that the result of authentic 'Jesus dreams' is that men and women long to read the Bible. That e-mail I quoted earlier went straight on to say, 'I would like to receive a Bible and some teaching.'

I had a sad experience visiting a church once. We all heard a strong and clear sermon on a wonderful Bible passage (I think it was from Luke 15). But at the end of the sermon the leader of the meeting said, 'Now I want to know whether God is speaking to us.' By this he did not mean, 'Were you listening to the sermon? Have you been touched by the Word of God and moved to respond?' He meant, 'Does anyone have a word of knowledge or prophecy to share with us?' His question was the prompt for various 'words' which, whether or not they were genuine (no doubt there will be differing opinions about that), were completely unrelated to the Bible passage. I naively thought God had spoken to us in the Bible; the impression was given that this was not so.

Any authentic experience of God that is indirectly the result of the Bible ought to whet in us a healthy appetite to get that message directly from the Bible. If it does not, we must question its authenticity. And, of course, God is God, and is well able to reveal Himself in any way He chooses. All through the Old Testament period He revealed Himself through dreams and visions. Who is to say that He cannot sometimes, in exceptional circumstances, use that Old Testament pattern today? But in view of the complete revelation of the Father in Christ, we will not long for those kinds of revelation. We have access in the Bible to Christ through Scripture, and in Christ we have the Father fully made known to us. That is a higher, fuller and better revelation.

TRUTH MATTERS

Christopher Hitchens (the atheist brother of Peter Hitchens), in his book *God is not great: how religion poisons everything*, which is an aggressive diatribe against all religions, tells of how he explored what he calls the 'Eastern' solution, by visiting the ashram of a celebrated guru in Poone in the hills above Mumbai. At the entrance to the tent where the guru taught was a notice which read, 'Shoes and minds must be left at the gate'.[8] He rightly

---

8   Christopher Hitchens, *God is not great* (London: Atlantic Books, 2007), p. 195f

mocks the nonsense of being asked to leave his mind behind at the gate. For truth matters. The so-called new atheists represent an intriguing revolt against post-modernism. They agree that truth matters. We will agree with them about that. They just don't think Christianity is true.

Plenty of people don't care about truth. One social observer has suggested that the four characteristic questions of recent generations are as follows. Those born before about 1945 he calls the Pre-Boomer generation. Their question is the old question, 'Is it true?' Those born from the end of the Second World War up to about 1964 are often called the Baby Boomer Generation. Their concern is pragmatic. They ask 'Does it work?' After that comes what is sometimes called 'Generation X'. They are the consumers. They ask, 'Do I want it?' And now, what he calls the Millennial generation. Their concern is with image. They ask 'Will I look good if I buy into this belief?'

I'm sure that's an oversimplification. But there is something in the observation that questions of truth are less prominent today than once they were. Coming back from a conference once, I had to get a taxi to the station. I tried rather incompetently to talk to the taxi driver about Jesus, and he said, 'I'll tell you what I think about Jesus… top bloke, really top bloke, went around healing people (more of a doctor really), and then the stories about him grew… rather like Princess Diana… in 2,000 years Jesus will be "Diana"…' When I offered to send him a Bible so that he could look at the evidence, he said there was no point as he wouldn't read it. But the old question, 'Is it true?' won't go away. It is the only question which provides an anchor through the storms of life.

It is frightening how easily we Christians give others the impression that they ought to leave their minds at the church door and slip into mysticism. For example, we are often guilty of using a shallow analogy when speaking of having a personal relationship with God. So we might hear someone claim, 'Of course, God talks to me directly. That is what a personal relationship is. What an odd relationship it would be if He didn't talk to me.' But then suppose we mischievously replied, 'Why, of course, my friend. And no doubt you see God too?' And suppose they replied, 'Of course I see Him. What an odd friendship it would be if I didn't see Him.' We will probably say, 'My friend, you are hallucinating. Go and see a psychiatrist.'

MYSTICISM LEADS TO LIBERALISM

It is also frightening how close such Christian mysticism is to liberalism. If a subjective experience is the driving force of our discipleship, we will be vulnerable, for it will only be our own emotional energy that keeps us going. As someone has said, when such people 'run out of emotional energy, they become Liberals.'[9] In his book *Christianity and Liberalism* (1923) J. Gresham Machen writes against liberals who said that Christianity is 'a life rather than doctrine' and that we should mind more about living the Christian life than arguing about creeds and doctrines. On the contrary, he points out, 'a creed is not a mere expression of Christian experience, but ... it is a setting forth of those facts upon which experience is based'. To say that 'Christianity is a life, not a doctrine' 'has an appearance of godliness' but 'is radically false.'[10]

Again, Machen defends Christianity against the liberal assault on the doctrine of the objective atonement won by Jesus on the Cross. The liberal criticises salvation by the Cross because 'it is dependent upon history.' It is not so much what Christ did long ago that matters, they say, but what He does now for the Christian. But, Machen points out, this

'involves a total abandonment of the Christian faith. If the saving work of Christ were confined to what He does now for every Christian, there would be no such thing as a Christian gospel – an account of an event which put a new

---

9   Peter Adam (Personal correspondence, quoted with permission)

10   J. Gresham Machen, *Christianity and Liberalism* (new edition. Grand Rapids, Michigan: Eerdmans, 2009), p. 17

The Spirit and other spirits

face on life. What we should be left with would be simply mysticism, and *mysticism is quite different from Christianity. It is the connection of the present experience of the believer with an actual historic appearance of Jesus in the world which prevents our religion from being mysticism and causes it to be Christianity*[11].

AN ILLUSTRATION FROM CHURCH HISTORY: THE QUAKERS

Let me comment on this briefly from church history. In his book *Hearing God's words*, Peter Adam has a superb section on the debates between the Puritans and the Quakers in the 1650s. [12] The Quakers began as Puritans who were dissatisfied with their experience of God, frustrated by church structures, found the Bible a cold and dead book and longed for something more.

The root question was, how does God speak, or, as we might say, the relationship between the Spirit and the Word. Is the Bible the Spirit's sword and book, or does the Spirit speak immediately to the individual apart from the Bible? In a way, it is Joyce Huggett and Jack Deere before their time.[13] But it is sobering to see how Quakerism developed. Before long, they denied that God spoke through the Bible at all. So these questions of word and Spirit are very significant.

The new Bible Speaks Today book on *The Message of the Holy Spirit* seems to me to misrepresent the ministry of the Spirit in a dangerous way. The author tells us that the Spirit is our personal mentor and intimate friend who 'sometimes… speaks through the Bible' but also in many other ways, entirely independent of the Bible. Our challenge, we are told 'is that we do not slip into exclusively using the Bible as our guide, forgetting that the Spirit who inspired and preceded it also

---

11   Ibid., p. 102 (my italics)

12   Peter Adam, *Hearing God's words* (New Studies in Biblical Theology. Leicester: IVP/Apollos, 2004), pp. 179-202; see also Peter Adam, *Written for Us* (Nottingham: IVP, 2008), pp. 234-7

13   Joyce Huggett, *Listening to God* (2nd Edition, London: Hodder & Stoughton, 1996), Jack Deere, *Surprised by the Voice of God* (Grand Rapids, Michigan: Zondervan, 2006)

speaks outside it as well as through it.' So instead of reading and hearing the Bible too much we ought to listen in silence for His voice[14]. This sounds pious, but looks to me to be on a trajectory towards Quakerism.

I read a review of a book by two Oxford scholars whose central thesis is that 'discerning the voice of God should be done by subordinating the text of the Bible to our perception of what the Spirit is now saying in our current circumstances.'[15] Not surprisingly, their conclusions differed sharply from apostolic Christianity. This is how the process works, when we leave historic Christianity and move towards mysticism. First we say that our experience needs to supplement the revelation of the Bible, and in the next generation we say that the Bible must be subordinated to our experience.

CONCLUSION

Luther distinguished the external clarity of Scripture from its internal clarity.[16] External clarity is what any linguistically competent reader can understand. Internal clarity is the response of the heart to the truth of Christ in Scripture (which is the subject of chapter 7). It is very important that we maintain the direction of movement from external clarity to internal clarity, from out to in. In a perceptive article, Jonathan Mumme has noted that, 'Any internal clarity is by way of the Holy Spirit working through these external means.' Mumme goes on to observe that, 'If things don't go from out to in, they go from in to out' which is what happened with Luther's fanatical opponents in the so-called Radical Reformation[17].

---

14   Keith Warrington, *The Message of the Holy Spirit* (Bible Speaks Today. Nottingham: IVP, 2009), pp. 195, 205, 245f

15   Review by Gwilym Davies of *The Bible for Sinners*, Christopher Rowland and Jonathan Roberts (London: SPCK, 2008) in 'Churchman' 124/2 Summer 2010

16   See pp. 111-12

17   Jonathan Mumme, 'The Spirit, the Spirits, and the Letter: Martin Luther on the Holy Spirit and the Holy Scriptures' in *Modern Reformation,* vol. 19:6 (Escondido: White Horse Inn)

The Spirit and other spirits

Christianity is not mysticism. But it can very easily metamorphose into a thinly Christianised mysticism. When it does, it is only one generation away from abandoning Christian orthodoxy. Jesus told the apostles that it was necessary for them to bear testimony because they – and they alone – had been with Him from the beginning of that wonderful public ministry in which He made the Father known. It is through their word, their reliable Spirit-led testimony to Jesus Christ, that we come to authentic faith. And it is through being anchored to, and fed by, their witness in Scripture, that we are kept in faith in Christ.

Let us never slip into speaking of the Bible as a dead book. Back in 1923 J. Gresham Machen wrote, 'Let it not be said that dependence upon a book is a dead or an artificial thing. The Reformation of the sixteenth century was founded upon the authority of the Bible, yet it set the world aflame. Dependence upon a word of man would be slavish, but dependence upon God's word is life'[18]. Elsewhere he speaks of 'a "dead orthodoxy" (so called) that is pulsating with life in every word. In such orthodoxy there is life enough to set the whole world aglow with Christian love'.[19]

STUDY AND DISCUSSION QUESTIONS

1. Read John 15:26, 27 again. Why do we deduce that the two testimonies to Jesus must be of different kinds?

2. What was the old debate about the 'Jesus of history' and the 'Christ of faith' all about? What are the implications of this today?

3. Why is being anchored in the Bible the only way for the church to be useful to a needy world?

4. What was the point of the story of 'doubting Thomas'?

---

18   J. Gresham Machen, *Christianity and Liberalism* (new edition. Grand Rapids, Michigan: Eerdmans, 2009), p. 67

19   Ibid., p. 39

5. What does it mean in practice not to believe every spirit (1 John 4:1)? By what objective criteria do we discern which is the Spirit of truth?

6. Why does mysticism lead away from genuine Christianity?

7

The Spirit at work in the world and the church

Who will convince men and women that Jesus and the gospel of Jesus is true? Who will bring home to minds, hearts, consciences and wills the reality of the Father God? Who will bear witness to Jesus as He makes the Father God known? I can read my Bible or I can teach and preach the Bible with humility, accuracy, faithfulness, confidence, courage and passion, and yet nothing happens, to me or to others. It can remain just truths that stay outside of the hearts of us all. While Christianity is not fluid, subjective mysticism, neither is it bare history. In chapter 2 we learned the sobering truth that until the Spirit was poured out, even the flawless earthly ministry of Jesus Christ was a failure. Until and unless the Spirit moves upon human hearts, no one repents and no one believes. So let us go back to that remarkable double testimony with which we started chapter 6,

> 'When the Counsellor comes, whom I will send to you from
> the Father, the Spirit of truth who goes out from the Father,
> he will testify about me. And you also must testify, for you
> have been with me from the beginning.' (John 15:26, 27)

In chapter 6 we considered the vital importance of the apostolic testimony. Now we turn to the other witness, the Spirit of truth.

We saw in chapter 6 that this double testimony only makes sense if the Spirit's witness is of a different and complementary kind to that of the apostles. He does not supplement their inadequate witness, adding some information they failed to pass on. Indeed His testimony is primary and sovereign, for He is God the Holy Spirit. To take my illustration of the Wimbledon champion needing help on a tennis court, suppose that instead of being offered another tennis player, the champion were in need of a tennis *racket*. That would make much more sense. The racket does not supplement his inadequacy as a player; it is the instrument with which he plays. This is more in line with the picture we find of the Bible and the Spirit. The Bible is to the Spirit what the racket is to the champion, although the Bible's metaphor is the sword rather than the tennis racket! (Eph. 6:17)

WHY WE NEED THE SPIRIT'S TESTIMONY

In chapter 5, I spoke of authentic Christianity as being like a hiker walking on a high ridge. On the one side is the fall into mysticism, and from that to liberalism. But on the other side there is another danger, that Christianity will become a cold, dead, cerebral business with no life-changing power, what Dr Martyn Lloyd-Jones used to call 'an ossified orthodoxy'. In the early nineteenth century the Church of Scotland was orthodox, but one historian commented that, 'Preaching tended either towards mere morality divested of its spiritual basis, or the working out of an abstract and rigid doctrinal system which took little account of the changing wants and questionings of humanity.' One pastor complained that 'men know God only as a bundle of doctrines.' The historian comments that against this background, 'Fervent evangelicalism could not but be restless.'[1]

In his book *Stirrings of the Soul*, Michael Raiter speaks of the danger of having 'a creed we subscribe to rather than a person we belong to'. He suggests we sometimes behave as if the

---

1   Timothy C. F. Stunt, *From Awakening to Secession: Radical Evangelicals in Switzerland and Britain 1815-1835* (Edinburgh: T & T Clark, 2000), pp. 222, 235f

The Spirit at work in the world and the church

Westminster Shorter Catechism, instead of saying, 'The chief end of man is to glorify God and enjoy him for ever,' were to read, 'The chief end of man is to read the Bible and study it forever!'[2]

How do you keep a movement fresh? There is always something a little sad about walking round the home of a famous person from a past generation, perhaps Winston Churchill's home in Chartwell, Kent, or Abraham Lincoln's home in Springfield, Illinois. We took a group of overseas students on a tour of the Houses of Parliament recently. It was, for example, fascinating to stand in the chamber used by the House of Commons in 1940, where Churchill made his great parliamentary speeches. And yet there is something frustrating, a sense that these events are from a bygone age and unrecoverable. There is about these places, 'the sadness that hangs over the home of a great man where the small memorials of his particular being – his chair, his slippers, his spectacles are lovingly and sadly cherished by generations of his disciples'[3]. Somehow all we are left with are the great man's slippers, just relics of a bygone age. The movement may be historically true, but it is no longer experientially real.

It could so easily have been so with the Jesus movement. It was necessary that the Word should become flesh in one place at one time, so that what He said, was, did and suffered were part of public human history, witnessed, attested, genuine and factual. This was a revelation whose truth could be publicly known. But if the story had ended there, it would have become steadily more and more second-hand and remote. As it receded farther and farther into the past it would slip from our grasp. It would have become a museum piece. Christianity would amount to little more than philosophical principles and fading memories.

All we could do would be to think of Jesus 'from a worldly point of view' (2 Cor. 5:16), to visit the land where He walked

---

2   Michael Raiter, *Stirrings of the Soul: Evangelicals and the New Spirituality* (London: Good Book Company, 2003), p. 228

3   Lesslie Newbigin, *The Light has Come* (Grand Rapids, Michigan: Eerdmans, 1982), p. 210

and wish we had been there with Jesus. 'If only I had been in Galilee when He walked on water or stilled the storm,' we would say. 'If only I had been at the grave of Lazarus when Jesus called him from the dead.' I went to Israel, Sinai and the West Bank some years ago, and it was very interesting. But it wasn't a spiritual experience. I was no closer to God there than here. If someone thinks they will get closer to God by visiting Jerusalem, they are still thinking of Jesus 'from a worldly point of view'. We ought not to care *from a religious point of view* which religion controls Jerusalem, Bethlehem or Nazareth, because access to these places has no effect on our relationship with God. In 1869 two forthright Scottish Presbyterian sisters visited Jerusalem and saw some other Christians going to visit the grave of Christ. One of them wrote, 'we can hardly understand what benefit they expect to derive from visiting it. Our Saviour is risen, and the distance is short indeed which separates Him from a believing soul'[4]

But that is all there would be – just memories – were it not for the witness of the Spirit. When Mary Magdalene wanted to cling to the Risen Jesus He told her not to, because very soon He would ascend, and after that the Spirit would be poured out, and from then on a new relationship was created in which she and all the disciples could call God 'Father'. Things would never be the same again (John 20:11-18).

A student once said to a Christian speaker after an evangelistic talk: 'It seems to be true; but it doesn't seem real.' That was an interesting comment. He thought Christianity sounded true in a cold, logical way; it made sense, it fitted together, and he thought it held together in a reasonable way. But it didn't feel real in experience. The ministry of the Holy Spirit is to take what seems true in an outward sense and to make it true in an inward sense, real in experience. There is no real Christian experience apart from the ministry of the Holy Spirit. He is 'the Spirit of truth'.

---

4   Janet Soskice, *Sisters of Sinai* (London: Chatto and Windus, 2009), p. 52

The Spirit at work in the world and the church

A friend of mine used to tell the story of when he took a youth group round the waxworks at Madame Tussaud's in London. I think they may have been in the Chamber of Horrors. It was dark, he had been there before, and he was standing quietly lost in his thoughts, when he noticed a little knot of people around him looking for the notice which – they assumed – would tell them which historical figure he was. When he realised they thought he was an exhibit, he stayed still to enjoy the joke for a while. But then he sneezed, and they fell back in surprise, because, as he put it, for them a figure of history had become a figure of life.

So we now ask what kind of testimony the Holy Spirit gives to Jesus Christ, and how we may hear and experience His divine witness. I want to consider the Spirit's testimony under four headings: Conviction, Leading, Warning, and Equipping for Mission.

1. Conviction of truth

So far we have considered two promises of Jesus about the Spirit (John 14:26 and John 16:12-15). In each case we have seen that it is a promise for the apostles. We shall consider below a secondary sense in which these promises may also apply to us. But in this same section of John's Gospel, there is a clear promise concerning the ministry of the Spirit, that is directed to 'the world' rather than to the apostles,

> 'When he (the Spirit) comes, he will convict the world of guilt in regard to sin and righteousness and judgement: in regard to sin, because men do not believe in me; in regard to righteousness, because I am going to the Father, where you can see me no longer; and in regard to judgement, because the prince of this world now stands condemned.' (John 16:8-11)

The Spirit has a ministry and testimony of conviction[5]. By nature the world responds to the apostolic witness the way that the unbelieving Jews responded to Isaiah's ministry, which

---

5   David Jackman has written helpfully on this ministry in *Spirit of Truth* (Ross-shire: Christian Focus/PT Media, 2006), pp. 53-7

was to them like a sealed book, and they were like people who cannot read (Isa. 29:11, 12). We respond as they did to Jesus Himself. In spite of His flawless words and mighty works, still they would not believe (John 12:37). The promise of John 16:8-11 comes immediately after a section (John 15:18–16:4) focusing on the hostility of the world to Jesus and His apostles. In this context, the Spirit conducts Jesus' law-suit.

He is not guiding the world. He is not leading the world into truth. This is not 'Creation Spirituality' in which Mother Earth has some kind of evolving consciousness. No, His ministry is to convince the world that it is wrong. The only work the Bible says the Spirit of God does in the world is to bring conviction. He takes the objective, historical, apostolic testimony to Jesus and places it against the unbelieving heart. Like a successful prosecutor, He will bring home to the heart that awful sinking feeling, like the feeling a motorist gets when he sees a flashing blue light in the mirror while speeding.

He brings conviction of sin, 'because men do not believe in me'. This probably means not just that unbelief in Jesus is a sin (though it is), but that unbelief in Jesus proves and exposes sin. If a prophet speaks to me, I can always find some reason for rejecting what he says. Always there is something wrong with the preacher or the messenger, and so I can find an excuse for ignoring them. But when a perfect man preaches to me and I reject and hate Him, I show that I have no excuse and my sin is exposed.

Second, He brings a conviction about righteousness 'because I am going to the Father'. This probably means that when God raises Jesus from the dead, He reverses the world's verdict on Him. The world thought Jesus was unrighteous, and that is why they crucified Him. But when He goes to the Father, the world's verdict is turned upside down and it is publicly seen that Jesus is righteous. The Spirit convicts the world that Jesus is righteous, and therefore, by implication, that we are not.

Third, he brings conviction about judgement 'because the prince of this world now stands condemned.' The prince of this world, Satan, who stands at the pinnacle of all this world's value systems, is shown up to be utterly evil and condemned, when he crucifies the righteous Jesus. The Spirit brings conviction of this. By nature I thought the world's values were valid and I took my values from the world. The Spirit convinces me how utterly wrong I was.

So, in summary, I thought I was OK; I thought that Jesus was irrelevant; I thought the world was a great place to find my values. The Spirit makes me put up my hands and admit that I am deeply not OK, that Jesus is the only really right person in history, and the world is walking on its head. He convicts me of my sin, of Jesus' righteousness and the world's judgement.

This is the convincing and convicting work we see in evidence in Thessalonica. In his first letter to this young church, Paul writes,

> 'For we know, brothers loved by God, that he has chosen you, because our gospel came to you not simply with words, but also with power, with the Holy Spirit and with deep conviction.' (1 Thess. 1:4, 5)

The gospel of Jesus did come in words (it always does)[6]; but it did not come 'simply with words'. It came with words; these words were the objective words of the apostolic testimony to Jesus. But those words were accompanied by the necessary and complementary work of the Spirit who brought those words to bear upon their hearts with power so that there was a full conviction that the apostolic gospel was true. First He brought the gospel to bear on the hearts of the preachers, so that they themselves were deeply convinced that their message was true. And then He brought their words to bear on their hearers. He convinced people through convinced people.[7] This is the work

6   For a helpful discussion of the connection between rationality and the convicting work of the Spirit, with its implications for Christian apologetics, see John M. Frame, 'The Spirit and the Scriptures' in D. A. Carson and John D. Woodbridge (eds.), *Hermeneutics, Authority and Canon* (Leicester: IVP, 1986), pp. 229-35

7   As Dr Martyn Lloyd-Jones famously expressed it, 'Preaching is theology coming through a man who is on fire!' It is 'Logic on Fire! Eloquent Reason' – D. M. Lloyd-Jones, *Preaching and Preachers* (London: Hodder and Stoughton, 1971), pp. 88, 97

of the Spirit. He does not add fresh information beyond the apostolic gospel; but He persuades men and women that this gospel is true. 'The Spirit does not whisper to us special reasons that are not otherwise available; rather, He opens our eyes to acknowledge those that *are* available...'.[8]

In Hebrews 3 and 4, the writer of the letter expounds a text in Psalm 95, prefacing it with the words, 'as the Holy Spirit says'. This text includes the words, 'Today, if you hear his voice, do not harden your hearts'. The word 'today' is at the heart of what he says. The voice of God had been heard by the people of Israel during the wilderness wanderings when He told them to enter the promised land and they refused. Then, many years later, when the Psalm was written, the same appeal was made not to harden their hearts. The writer brings that text straight into the present. It applies 'as long as it is called Today' (Heb. 3:13), which is a wonderful way of saying that the word of God by which He spoke in the past is precisely the word of God by which the Holy Spirit 'says' (present tense) today and every day. The past-tense word is the present-tense word. We do not need a new word for the present. What we need is for the Spirit of God to bring a deep heart-conviction to us that the past-tense word is true and 'penetrates even to dividing soul and spirit, joints and marrow' and 'judges the thoughts and attitudes of the heart' today (Heb. 4:12, 13).

We cannot do this convincing work for ourselves or for others by our preaching, our witness, our apologetics or our lives. When William Wilberforce persuaded his good friend Pitt the Younger to hear a sermon from a noted evangelical preacher, Richard Cecil, Pitt said afterwards, 'You know, Wilberforce, I have not the slightest idea what that man has been talking about'.[9] People can be completely untouched by

---

8   John M. Frame, 'The Spirit and the Scriptures' in D. A. Carson and John D. Woodbridge (eds.), *Hermeneutics, Authority and Canon* (Leicester: IVP, 1986), p. 232

9   William Hague *William Wilberforce* (London: HarperCollins, 2007), p. 103

everything Christians say and do. Only the Spirit can bring this conviction.

The missionary David Brainerd wrote in his diary: 'I longed for the Spirit of preaching to descend and rest upon ministers, that they might address the consciences of men with closeness and power.'[10] This is exactly what happened to the apostles after Pentecost. As John Chrysostom put it, after 'they had received the Spirit' they changed and, 'the Spirit made them men of iron instead of men of clay, gave them wings, and allowed them to be cast down by nothing human.'[11] They were arrested and made to stand trial before 'governors and kings as witnesses to them.' Jesus had told them not to worry because, 'At that time you will be given what to say, for it will not be you speaking, but the Spirit of your Father speaking through you' (Matt. 10:18-20). And this is what happened.

Professor David Wells says that, 'Outside the supernatural workings of God's Spirit, unbelief is invincible, cultures are impenetrable, and doors are closed.' But when He does His work of conviction, everything changes. Writing about a remarkable work of God in New England in the early eighteenth century, Jonathan Edwards wrote that, 'The arguments are the same that they have heard hundreds of times; but the force of the arguments, and their conviction by them, is altogether new; they come with a new and before unexperienced power. Before, they heard it was so, and they allowed it to be so; but now they see it to be indeed so. Things now look exceedingly plain to them, and they wonder they did not see them before.'[12]

How badly we need this ministry. Alexander Whyte (1836-1921) wrote about preaching to the conscience: 'Spiritual preaching; real face to face, inward, verifiable, experimental, spiritual preaching – that kind of preaching is scarcely ever

10   Iain Murray *The Old Evangelicalism* (Edinburgh: Banner of Truth, 2005), p. 30f

11   John Chrysostom, *Homily LXXV on John's Gospel* (part 5)

12   Jonathan Edwards, 'A Narrative of Surprising Conversions' in *Jonathan Edwards on Revival* (Edinburgh: Banner of Truth, 1991), p. 43

heard in our day. There is great intellectual ability in the pulpit of our day, great scholarship, great eloquence, and great earnestness, but spiritual preaching, preaching to the spirit – "wet-eyed" preaching – is a lost art.' He went on to say, 'Unless (your minister) strikes terror and pain into your conscience every Sabbath, unless he makes you tremble every Sabbath under the eye and hand of God, he is no true minister to you.'[13] However much we may long for this kind of preaching, we need to remember that such preaching cannot be humanly engineered by a change of style. It is the sovereign work of the Spirit of God, who sometimes chooses to work in powerful conviction upon the hearers even when the speaker is deeply inadequate, even passionless and dull. This is not an excuse for being passionless and dull, but it is a reaffirmation that the Spirit is sovereign and works through the word He inspired, whenever and upon whomever He chooses. We must pray for this sovereign work of the Spirit.

The conviction that comes from the Spirit is a hallmark of real Christianity. When Philipp Melanchthon was uncertain about whether some people who had professed faith were genuine, Luther wrote to him, 'In order to explore their individual spirit' (that is, whether they are genuine or not), '… you should inquire whether they have experienced spiritual distress and the divine birth, death and hell. If you should hear that all [their experiences] are pleasant, quiet, devout (as they say), and spiritual, then don't approve them, even if they should say they were caught up to the third heaven.'[14] It is a bracing test. When we hear someone tell their story, if there is no trace of conviction of sin, of the misery of guilt and the longing to have that guilt made clean, we may reasonably ask whether the experience they describe is real Christianity.

---

13 Quoted in Iain Murray *The Old Evangelicalism* (Edinburgh: Banner of Truth, 2005), p. 36

14 Quoted in Ibid., p. 24

So this work of the Spirit is a very important and wonderful work. And we need to pray for it to happen. We cannot do this work. Someone has said that evangelism is like a man with a box of matches trying to light leaves in a dark damp valley. Usually there is no response, occasionally a flicker. And then he finds a leaf dried and warmed by God's wind and sunshine, and it lights.

2. Leading into the way of truth

In chapter 3 we considered the promise of John 14:26, in which Jesus promises the apostles that the Spirit will teach and remind them of what He had said. We saw that this promise must necessarily be to the apostles, since only they could be reminded; you and I today cannot be reminded of what we never heard from the lips of Jesus in His earthly ministry.

We also considered the promise of John 16:12-15, where Jesus promises the apostles that the Spirit will lead them into all truth, speaking to them the things of Christ, which are the things of the Father, so that they can unpack that great completed revelation for us. We have the fruit of that promise in the New Testament and ought to be deeply grateful for this ministry of the Spirit.

Both John 14:26 and John 16:12-15 are promises for the apostles. They give us strong encouragement to trust the New Testament. The New Testament is the primary fulfilment of these promises of Jesus that the Spirit would lead the apostles into the whole truth about Jesus. They were gloriously fulfilled in the apostles' lives and their preaching, which we have recorded for us in the New Testament. For the New Testament is the written-down preaching of the apostles, who were led by the Spirit into all truth. So the New Testament is an utterly trustworthy and sufficient testimony to Jesus, to lead us into the knowledge of Jesus, and thereby to make the Father known to us.

But many will object to this. Surely, they will say, when we read the rest of John 14–16, we quite naturally assume that most of it is applicable not just to the apostles, but also to disciples of every age. For example, immediately after the promise of John 14:26 to the apostles we hear Jesus say,

> 'Peace I leave with you; my peace I give you. I do not give to you as the world gives. Do not let your hearts be troubled and do not be afraid' (John 14:27).

It would seem strange to us to claim that this promise of peace extended only to the apostles. It is a fair objection. So let us ask what derivative application there may be from the promises of John 14:26 and John 16:12-15, to disciples today.

First, John 14:26. Although the Spirit can only remind the apostles of what Jesus has taught them during His earthly ministry, He can presumably remind us of what we may have read or heard from the Bible. That too is a wonderful ministry. But all He is doing is reminding us today of precisely the same truths that He first reminded the apostles. He reminded the apostles what Jesus had spoken from the Father. He now reminds us of what He had reminded the apostles. This 'reminding' is more than just bringing Scripture to our minds, though it includes that. Like all biblical remembering, it involves response. As David Jackman puts it, 'Biblical remembering is always rehearsing what has been said or done in the past with a view to present action.' As he points out, we think of remembering in the same way ourselves: 'Just imagine telling your wife that you remembered your wedding anniversary last week but did nothing more than make a mental note of it!'[15] So when the Holy Spirit reminds us of the truth of Jesus as given to the apostles, He spurs us into action, a fresh repentance, a renewed faith and a new obedience.

Similarly with John 16:12-15. The Spirit does lead His people of every generation to walk in the truth as it was revealed in Jesus. But the truth He leads us into, is precisely the same truth into which He led the apostles. The Jesus He leads us to know is exactly the same Jesus He led them to know. The Father

---

15   David Jackman, *Spirit of Truth* (Ross-shire: Christian Focus/PT Media, 2006), p. 134

The Spirit at work in the world and the church

He makes known to us is precisely the same Father He made known to the apostles. As David Jackman has put it,

> 'He does not reveal new truth, but leads us into the whole truth which is already set forth in Jesus' above whom 'there could be no fuller revelation of God's truth'.

> 'The Holy Spirit does not set us free to wander into new realms of "revelation", secretly given or privately received. For the power of the Spirit is not revealed in secret, mystical messages given to a few super-spiritual people. His power is seen in the proclamation of Jesus Christ as the way, the truth and the life…'[16]

So it is not that the Spirit supplements the incompleteness or imperfection of the apostles' testimony to Christ; rather He takes their complete and sufficient objective testimony and makes it effective in the subjectivities of our hearts and lives so that we understand and are led in the Way.

This is not, therefore, a promise that the synods or councils of the church will be led into new and different truth. As a friend of mine wrote, 'No spiritual experience can transcend heterodoxy in faith and morality (as "the Holy Spirit will lead you into all truth" has been sometimes misinterpreted in terms of "a shared spiritual experience is primary – a common doctrinal agreement can wait!")'[17]. Nor is it a promise that the individual believer will enjoy private revelations. It is a promise to the apostles wonderfully fulfilled in the writing of the New Testament.

This understanding fits with what we see the Spirit doing in the rest of the New Testament. It does not seem that He goes on adding extra revelations, additional theological informational downloads year by year. And He certainly does not correct earlier misinformation and lead the church to change its mind, as is often suggested today. No, what He does is guide the people of God to walk in the way of truth revealed in Jesus to

16   Ibid., p57f, and see the whole section pp. 57-62

17   Paul Perkin, personal correspondence, quoted with permission

the apostles by the Spirit. Elsewhere this is called the 'fruit' of the Spirit in godly, Christlike living (Gal. 5:22, 23). The Spirit produces fresh fruit but not fresh revelations.

The great Puritan writer John Owen wrote that the Spirit, 'reveals to the souls of sinners the good things of the covenant of grace, which the Father has provided, and the Son purchased. He shows to us mercy, grace, forgiveness, righteousness, acceptance with God'; He 'makes them know' these things 'for their own good – know them as originally the things of the Father, prepared from eternity in his love and goodwill; as purchased for them by Christ, and laid up in store in the covenant of grace for their use. Then is Christ magnified and glorified in their hearts; then they know what a Saviour and Redeemer he is'.[18]

So we must pray, and depend on the Spirit. Without His gracious ministry we cannot grasp any spiritual truth, we cannot know Jesus, the Father will not be made known to us, and we will understand nothing of the Bible. We need Him to shed His light on the page and into our hearts.

We need to distinguish the ministry of the Spirit in inspiring and supervising the writing and preservation of Scripture from His ministry to believers today. We believe God breathed out the Scriptures through the Spirit who is His 'breath' (2 Tim. 3:16), that people were carried along by the Spirit as they wrote and spoke (2 Pet. 1:21), and that He sovereignly supervised the writing and preservation of Scripture. But He also drives Scripture home to human hearts, 'breathing' that word into our hearts today. The technical terms theologians sometimes use are inspiration and illumination. It is very important to keep these distinct in our minds. Inspiration is what the Spirit did for the apostles and apostolic writers of the New Testament. He breathed into them so that they wrote exactly what God wanted them to write.

He does not inspire us in the same way, as if we had a personal hotline to heaven. What He does for us is 'illumination' – that is,

---

18   John Owen, (Kelly M. Kapic and Justin Taylor (eds.)) *Communion with the Triune God* (Wheaton, Illinois: Crossway, 2007), p. 377

The Spirit at work in the world and the church

He shines His light in our hearts, opens our blind eyes, breathes His word into our hearts, so that we see and grasp what He has inspired the apostles to teach. His work in believers today and the church today is not therefore an independent, separate or supplementary work in adding to the revelation He has given in the Bible; it is a work of breathing into our hearts the breath or word He first taught the apostles.

Reading the Bible has been compared to viewing a stained-glass window. Without the Spirit, we are like those viewing the window from outside the unlit building. All we can see is darkness. But when the Spirit shines His light, it is as if we have come inside the building and can see the window in all its colours and beauty.

We must be careful not to confuse the Spirit's work of inspiration (of the writers) with His work of illumination (of the readers), as the famous twentieth-century theologian Karl Barth did. Barth argued that the Bible itself is not the Word of God, for it would compromise God's sovereignty (he suggested) if He had tied Himself to not contradicting words on a page. Rather, he said, the Bible sometimes becomes the Word of God when the Spirit breathes afresh upon it.[19] This weak understanding of Scripture came to be part of what is called neo-orthodoxy (which is really not orthodoxy at all.)

In saying this, Barth opened the door to every movement from Christianity to mysticism. For a perception of the Spirit's work that is independent of the text is rootless and without an anchor in the truth of Jesus as the Christ come in the flesh in human history. But God's sovereignty is not compromised by the authority of Scripture. Rather, as the theologian John Frame puts it,

'the sovereignty and freedom of God in the Spirit's testimony are seen, not in God's ability to contradict or modify or add to His

---

19 For a helpful outline and critique of Barth's doctrine of Scripture and the Spirit, see John M. Frame, 'The Spirit and the Scriptures' in D. A. Carson and John D. Woodbridge (eds.), *Hermeneutics, Authority and Canon* (Leicester: IVP, 1986), pp. 221-5

Word, but in His ability to drive it home to otherwise unwilling hearts, and indeed, to do everything He says He will do.[20]

The Spirit breathed out the Scriptures. And the Spirit works on us the hearers so that the word breathed into our hearts is powerful and effective to change us. Again and again in Paul's letters he prays, and tells us to pray, for the Spirit to give understanding (e.g. 1 Cor. 2:12; 2 Cor. 4:4-15; Eph. 1:17-19; Phil. 1:9-11; Col. 1:9-13). And understanding is always more than head knowledge, but includes response.

The Spirit is not a supplement to the written word, changing or adding to its meaning. Rather, He draws out its true and original meaning, in the light of the finished work of Christ. This distinction is important. It is sometimes suggested that the Spirit is the creative power who 'fuses' my horizon with the horizon of the text, thus creating some new meaning. By making 'this' mean 'that' He keeps Scripture fresh and relevant to the church in every age. So, on this understanding, the meaning does not reside in the Bible text, but in the encounter between the text and the Spirit-led reader or the Spirit-guided church. On this understanding, there is no such thing as a fixed, stable answer to the question, 'what does this text mean?' Instead the Spirit, working among the people of God leads us on beyond the literal meaning of the text and into a new abundance of creative meaning. In effect, therefore, the Spirit supplements the static deficiency of the letter of the word.

What then happens is that the authority of the word is effectively replaced by what is called the authority of God the Spirit, but is actually the authority of the interpretive community who claim the leading of the Spirit. Thus tradition creeps in by the back door and trumps the word.

The correct understanding, I believe, is this. The Spirit breathes into our hearts the Word He first breathed out from the Father. There is a stable meaning in the text. What it said, it says. What God spoke, He speaks. It has a fixed meaning.

---

20   Ibid., p. 225

The Spirit at work in the world and the church

That meaning is discerned by the usual conventions for understanding language and genre, in the overall context of the canon (see ch. 5). The Spirit does not change that meaning. He is not a rival author to the word. He is neither a second source of revelation nor a supplement to the word.

He works in the hearer, to change the hearer, not upon the word to change the word. He speaks only what He hears (John 16:13); He opens the ear of the hearer to hear what he or she has heard; and He redirects the heart of the hearer so that he or she turns and goes the way of the word.

So, for example, the Word issues a warning; the Spirit works on the believer to heed the warning. The Word gives a promise; the Spirit works in the believer's heart to live in the light of that promise. He brings the significance of the word to bear upon the hearer. He does not change the meaning of the word; but He charges it with contemporary significance. He shines His light on the word so that we understand it aright; He ministers to us its meaning. He does not change the sense, but He restores us to our senses. And He sanctifies the reader so that our hearts are turned to go the way the text points. The natural person does not accept the things of the Spirit of God, for they are spiritually discerned (1 Cor. 2:14). This does not mean that the unbeliever cannot understand the meaning of the Bible at all; he can, if he has linguistic competence in language and genre. But it means he will not go the way of its significance. He will not respond with the obedience of faith.

So the Spirit does not supplement the *sufficiency* of the word, but He works in us the *efficacy* of the word. He renders the word effective. The Spirit is, in a sense, mute without the word. But on the other hand the word is inactive without the Spirit. The word does not work on its own, as it were *ex opere operato*; it works as the Spirit renders it effective.

The Spirit does more in the believer than just to enable us to understand. He both opens our eyes to understand and warms our hearts to desire. He changes and redirects our affections. An important part of the Spirit's ministry is not so much making complex truths clear, as making ignored truth beautiful. When the Spirit works upon us and in us, 'We recognize the *loveliness* of the gospel and respond with joy'.[21]

Writing about Augustine, Peter Sanlon says,

> 'Augustine believed that the Spirit's role is to transform listeners – not primarily by helping them understand what they previously did not grasp, but by making them long passionately for what the Gospel promises: "When the Spirit of God calls the human race, telling us what we ought to do and promising us what we ought to hope for, he first makes us hot for the reward." (Sermon 16.1).'

Commenting on Romans 12:11, Augustine writes,

> 'Even now the fire is burning, the heat of the word is on, the fierce glow of the Holy Spirit... That heat belongs to the Holy Spirit, we are told by the apostle in Romans 12:11. So for the time being treat the Scripture of God as the face of God. Melt in front of it... Under the heat of the word, when the tears begin to flow, don't you feel yourself rather like wax beginning to drip and flow down as if in tears.' (Sermon 22.7).[22]

So the Spirit first convinces us of truth, and then leads us to walk in the way of truth.

3. Protection from error

Third, the Spirit protects the believer from error. In 1 John 2:20-27, John speaks of the Holy Spirit as the 'Anointing' possessed by all real believers. In the context where false teachers are trying to deceive them, he says,

> 'I am writing these things to you about those who are trying to lead you astray. As for you, the anointing you received from him remains in you, and you do not need anyone to teach you. But as his anointing teaches you about all things

---

21 Ibid., p. 234

22 Peter Sanlon, 'Depth and Weight: Augustine's Sermon Illustration' in *Churchman* 122/1 (Spring 2008), p. 71

and as that anointing is real, not counterfeit – just as it has
taught you, remain in him.' (1 John 2:26, 27)

There is an irony when John says 'you do not need anyone to
teach you.' He is teaching them that they don't need a teacher!
If he really thought Bible teachers were superfluous he wouldn't
write the letter. So what does he mean? Augustine puts it like this:

> 'There is here, my brothers, a great mystery on which to
> meditate: the sound of my voice strikes your ears, but the
> real Teacher is within. Do not think that anyone learns
> anything from another human being. We can draw your
> attention by the sound of our voice; but if within there is not
> the One who instructs, the noise of our words is in vain…
> The internal Master who teaches is Christ the Teacher; his
> inspiration teaches. Where his inspiration and anointing are
> not found, the external words are in vain.'[23]

The key point seems to be that even the youngest real believer
has within them the witness of the Spirit who warns them
against false teaching. Dr Martyn Lloyd-Jones comments,

> 'And thus it has often come to pass in the long history of the
> church that certain ignorant, more or less illiterate people
> have been able to discriminate between truth and error
> much better than the great doctors of the church. They were
> simple enough to trust the "anointing" and thus they were
> able to distinguish between things that differ.'[24]

Many of us know something of this in our own experience.
I remember as a young Christian at my university hearing a speaker
at the Christian Union. There seemed to be something not quite
right about what he was saying. I could not put my finger on what it
was, and if someone had explained it to me in doctrinal terms I am
not sure I would really have understood. I had not been a Christian
long. But I knew there was something wrong. That speaker later

---

23 Augustine, *Commentary on 1 John* in section on 1 John 2:26, 27

24 D. M. Lloyd-Jones, *Authority* (London: Inter-Varsity Fellowship, 1958), p. 79

became a thorn in the side of faithful evangelical Christians in his denomination. But I believe that it was the 'anointing', the presence and protecting ministry of the Spirit, which sounded a warning in me about him, even then. This is a much-needed, gracious work of the Spirit.

4. *Equipping for gospel mission*

The final ministry of the Spirit for us to consider is equipping the church for mission. In John 20:19-22 the church in embryo is promised the Spirit to equip them for the mission of gospel forgiveness. On the first Easter evening, the risen Lord stands in the midst of His church. These were not just the apostles. It is clear from the parallel passage in Luke (Luke 24:33-49, which refers to 'the Eleven and those with them') that others were there. This was a representative group of disciples, the church in embryo. Jesus sends them out:

'As the Father has sent me, I am sending you' (v. 21).

This does not mean that their mission is identical to Jesus' mission; it means that just as Jesus was a 'sent' person, sent by the Father, so they too are sent by Jesus. Then He breathes on them:

'Receive the Holy Spirit' (v. 22).

This seems to be an anticipatory trailer for the actual reception of the Spirit on the Day of Pentecost. D.A.Carson calls it, 'a kind of acted parable.'[25] This must be so, for there is no evidence that the disciples changed from frightened men and women into courageous missionary men and women until Pentecost, whereas from Pentecost onwards they did change gloriously.

And then Jesus tells them the substance and focus of their mission, which is to bring the declaration of gospel forgiveness to a needy world:

'If you forgive anyone his sins, they are forgiven; if you do not forgive them, they are not forgiven' (v. 23).

---

25   D. A. Carson, *The Gospel according to John* (Leicester: IVP, 1991), p. 655

The Spirit at work in the world and the church

Although Roman Catholic exegesis takes this text as a justification for the sacrament of priestly absolution, whereby an ordained priest can authoritatively and individually declare the forgiveness of sins, we ought to reject this exegesis. First, as we have noted, the group to which Jesus says this extends beyond the apostles, quite apart from excluding poor Thomas, who would thereby be excluded from this ministry. And second, there is no evidence in Acts or anywhere else in the New Testament that Christian leaders of any kind claimed to be able to exercise that kind of individual forgiving authority. They did not understand Jesus' promise this way.

The authority Jesus gives to the church is the gospel authority to declare – not to individuals but to whole classes of people ('anyone… them…' is plural) – what kinds of people are forgiven and what kinds of people are not forgiven. As Jesus puts it in Luke 24:47, they are to preach repentance and the forgiveness of sins in His name, which is exactly what we see them doing in Acts.

This is how the *Book of Common Prayer* of the Church of England understands this. In the service of Morning Prayer the congregation confess their sins and the Presbyter leading the service says,

> 'Almighty God… hath given power and commandment to his Ministers, to declare and pronounce to his people, being penitent, the Absolution and Remission of their sins: He pardoneth and absolveth all them that truly repent and unfeignedly believe his holy Gospel. Wherefore let us beseech him to grant us true repentance and his Holy Spirit …'

The Presbyter declares and pronounces the forgiveness that is proclaimed in the gospel. He does not proclaim forgiveness to an individual, but to a class of people ('all them that truly repent …'). So the Holy Spirit is given to the whole people of God to equip them for the wonderful ministry of declaring the forgiveness of sins through the gospel.

CONCLUSION: THE SPIRIT'S INTERNAL TESTIMONY

In summary, the testimony of the apostles is external, objective and historical. The testimony of the Spirit is internal. As John Frame has put it,

'The internal testimony is not new revealed words… , nor is it a new saving act in history… Rather, in the internal testimony, the Spirit operates in our hearts and minds, in ourselves as subjects, to illumine and persuade us of the divine words and deeds.'[26]

The ministry of the Spirit is supernatural and absolutely essential if any genuine and lasting spiritual work is to be done. We desperately need Him to do His work of bringing conviction that the Bible is trustworthy and true, of leading Christian people to walk in the way of the Christ of the Bible, to warn us of false spiritualities and to equip us for the ministry of bringing the gospel of forgiveness to a needy world.

STUDY AND DISCUSSION QUESTIONS

1. What happens to Christianity without the Holy Spirit's inward testimony to Jesus Christ?

2. In what ways does Jesus promise that the Holy Spirit will bring conviction? What experience do you have of this convicting work, in yourself and in others?

3. What does 'leading into truth' mean for us today, and how is it different from what the Holy Spirit did for the apostles?

4. What experience do you have of the Holy Spirit helping you not only to understand the Bible, but to love what you find in the Bible?

5. When have you experienced the Spirit warning you against wrong teaching about Christ?

6. It is not easy to bring the gospel of forgiveness to others. When and how has the Spirit enabled you to do this, either individually or along with others?

---

26 John M. Frame, 'The Spirit and the Scriptures' in D. A. Carson and John D. Woodbridge (eds.), *Hermeneutics, Authority and Canon* (Leicester: IVP, 1986), p. 230f

Conclusion

Hearing the Spirit

Let us draw our study to a close. We began by thinking of the various reasons why we are concerned about the relationship between the Spirit and the Bible, whether it be an anxiety that we are missing out, a longing for a deeper walk with God, a frustration with powerlessness in Christian service or discontent in church life. Our argument has taken us, mainly through John's Gospel, a long way.

We began in chapter 1 by thinking about the unique and deeply awesome revelation of God the Father by Jesus Christ in His earthly ministry, death and resurrection. This is the foundation of all our study. Jesus came to make the Father known, and He did make the Father known, fully and wonderfully. If we are not gripped by the wonder and finality of Jesus, we will never feel the force of the biblical argument that follows. But we learned also about the significance of the words He spoke, and how those words, given by the Father in eternity and given afresh by the limitless anointing of the Spirit in His humanity, were the words of eternal life. It was by His words that He interpreted His miracles, gave His teaching, corrected His enemies, and above all taught us to understand

His Cross and resurrection. Those words become the enduring revelation of the Father when Jesus has ascended to heaven and is no longer on earth in bodily form.

Then in chapter 2 we considered the sad and sobering – but not unexpected – truth that Jesus' earthly revelation of the Father failed. He made the Father known and yet nobody saw the Father. Until the Cross, when sin was paid for and hearts cleansed, the Spirit could not be poured out into the hearts of men and women. And until the Spirit enters the heart, the heart is hard and cold and will not and cannot see the Father as revealed in Jesus.

In chapters 3 and 4 we developed the argument and gave our reasons for believing that in the Bible's words we have the authentic, faithful and complete testimony to Jesus and His words, and therefore the revelation of the Father. The Father is made known by Jesus, and Jesus is attested by the Bible. So it must be to the Bible we turn when we want to know the Father and go on knowing Him more and more deeply. Chapter 5 was a more technical chapter in which we paused to think more deeply about the implications of this for reading and understanding the Bible. In particular, we considered the Bible's completeness as testimony to Christ and therefore its intelligibility and stability of meaning. It means what it means. The meaning it had is the meaning it has.

Chapters 6 and 7 examined the complementary roles of the objective, historical testimony to Jesus in the Bible and the subjective testimony to Jesus by the Spirit. In chapter 6 we sought to guard ourselves against being seduced by mystical impersonations of Christianity. But in many ways chapter 7 is the climactic chapter of the study. There we studied what the ministry of the Spirit is today and how that ministry works graciously upon us to bring conviction that the objective testimony is true. I hope we ended chapter 7 with a deep longing to see and experience more of the Spirit's gracious ministry in ourselves and in others.

Conclusion

So, finally, we ask how we ought to respond to these truths, both in seeking to hear the Spirit and – for those of us entrusted with Bible speaking (preachers, Bible teachers, youth workers, school workers, cross-cultural missionaries, Sunday school teachers, and so on) – in seeking to speak with the Spirit.

First, if we have grasped the central burden of our study, the uniqueness of the revelation of the Father by Jesus, we will never expect the Spirit to work apart from the revelation of the Father through Jesus in the Spirit-given testimony to Jesus in the Bible. God is sovereign, and so God the Holy Spirit is free to work how and when He chooses. Nothing we say in this study is an attempt to limit Him. How foolish that would be! But the Spirit of God is the Spirit of Christ. He loves to bring glory to Jesus. He speaks only what He hears from the Father, which are the things He hears from Jesus Christ, just as Jesus spoke only the things He heard from the Father. It is He who inspired and supervised the whole Bible testimony to the revelation of the Father in Christ, and we should confidently expect Him to speak and work through that objective testimony.

This means that when we set ourselves to hear God speak, both individually and in our meetings, we will never de-centre the Bible. We will never say that we are getting too much Bible, or look to listen to God in separate and independent ways.

But, second, we need to consider the implications of the clarity of the Bible. The Bible means what the Bible meant, and that meaning is discernible, by the normal means of human communication – language, genre, context and canon. So we will not expect the Spirit to give us some new and mystical meaning that the original text did not and could not have meant. We will be attentive to the text, listening carefully to what it says. In that listening, we will not be arrogantly individualistic. We will be very grateful both that the ascended Christ has given gifts of teaching to His church (Eph. 4:11), and that He has given us brothers and sisters to read the Bible with us. Further, those brothers and sisters extend backwards in time right through the history of the church. So we will listen humbly to how our fellow Christians have read the Bible in the past, respecting Christian tradition as an often helpful guide and corrective against idiosyncratic interpretation.

Finally, however, we will not just read the Bible (or, for some of us, teach the Bible). For we will always remember the strange powerlessness even of the Lord Jesus in His earthly ministry, before the Spirit came. Etched into our hearts will be the fact that until the Spirit worked upon human hearts, even the Lord Jesus could speak the very words of God, work the awesome works of God and live the flawless life of God, to no effect. You and I can teach the Bible day and night. We can read the Bible attentively, carefully, accurately. But neither we nor anybody else will be affected by what we teach or read, until and unless the Spirit of God works.

And so we will give ourselves to pray. As Bible readers, we will cry to God that by His Holy Spirit He will work in us. We will not pray that He changes the Bible. We will pray that He changes us, to open our blind eyes and to soften our hard hearts.

We will pray that the Spirit will make us honest men and women. For we are not by nature honest about ourselves. Not one of us comes to the Bible as a blank slate. We come with prejudices. We expect to find in the Bible what we want to find. As someone said, 'It is very hard to persuade a man to believe something when his salary depends upon his not believing it.' We do not want the Bible to tell us things we do not like, and therefore by nature we are likely to screen out from the Bible what we do not like, and to find in it what affirms us as we are. We prefer to use the Bible as a mirror reflecting back to us our own prejudices. Graeme Goldsworthy points out that the command to the church to have the word of Christ dwelling richly amongst them is preceded by the command to put to death what is earthly in them (Col. 3:5, 16).[1] So we will pray for

---

1   Graeme Goldsworthy, *Gospel-centred Hermeneutics* (Nottingham: IVP/Apollos, 2006), p. 314

a supernatural work of the Spirit in us, to give us honesty about ourselves.

We will pray for the Spirit to humble us under the mighty hand of God. We will not arrogantly assume we have 'got the Bible right' on our own. We will ask our friends, whether they are contemporary friends or friends from past generations of the church. It is a bit like a sailor on the ocean, wanting to know where he is. He certainly believes that he is somewhere. If he has any sense he will not subscribe to the so-called post-modern fancy that so long as he is happy where he is, then his longitude and latitude are 'true for him'; it would not be wise to go to sea with a sailor like that! No, he believes that he is somewhere. But he is humble enough to realise that he needs to take all the bearings he can to make sure he knows as accurately as he can where he is. In the same way, a humble Bible reader and listener will use all the help he or she can get from others.

We will pray for the Spirit to make us quietly attentive to the Word of God. Some of us are like hyperactive schoolchildren, always wanting to interrupt the teacher and butt in with our own ideas. Others of us are like the proverbial schoolroom back row, texting their friends under the table rather than really listening. The Spirit will quieten our hearts and minds so that we really listen, and are prepared to find that the Bible says things we did not expect, and may not have wanted to find. But we will listen, for we know that the Bible will show us the authentic Jesus, and the authentic Jesus will make known to us the Father. We will listen not in a mystical way, expecting the Spirit to short-circuit the normal processes of human communication. Rather, we will listen attentively to grasp the meaning of the Bible, praying that the Spirit will give us this attentiveness. Writing scathingly of the sort of literary criticism which tells us more about the prejudices of the critic than about the text, C.S. Lewis wrote, 'Find out what the author actually wrote and what the hard words meant and what the allusions were to, and you have done far more for me than a hundred new interpretations

or assessments could ever do.'[2] We will tremble lest we distort
the Bible because we don't like what it says, remembering that
distortion comes not because we are not clever enough but
because we are full of sinful desires (as we find in 2 Pet. 2 and
3, see especially 3:16).

Above all, we will pray for the Spirit to work in us a glad
obedience to the Word of God. As the Father continues to
be made known, we will gladly surrender to His goodness and
grace, and walk in His way. And so the Spirit will lead us to walk
in the paths of truth, as we understand the Bible and then obey
what we understand.

For those of us entrusted with speaking for God in preaching
and Bible teaching, this business of praying for humble, honest,
attentive listening is all the more vital. God governs and leads
His people by teachers and preachers who are themselves first
taught by God through the Scriptures. Our model for this is the
Servant of the Lord of Isaiah,

> 'The Sovereign LORD has given me an instructed tongue,
> to know the word that sustains the weary.
> He wakens me morning by morning,
> wakens my ear to listen like one being taught.' (Isa. 50:4)

The church needs to learn the Bible from teachers who are
themselves taught by the Bible. We need preachers and teachers
who have the tongues of attentive listeners. Otherwise they will
not be worth listening to. Preachers of the word are Christ's
gift to His church (Eph. 4:11). But they are gifts to the church
because they are not tyrants, little popes distributed here and
there. They are gifts because they themselves are accountable
to the Chief Shepherd (1 Pet. 5:1-4), and they can only preach
as they themselves listen.

In our Bible listening we will neither be proud nor slothful.
To be proud is to have the false certainty that we have the

---

2   C. S. Lewis, *An Experiment in Criticism* (Cambridge: Cambridge University Press,
     1961), p. 121

Conclusion

Bible's meaning sewn up. To be slothful is to despair of ever understanding the Bible by the usual means. When we are lazy, we will either seek a mystical understanding and will falsely credit this to the Spirit (as in, 'the Spirit showed me that this passage means …'), or we will resign ourselves to an immature dependency on our favourite teachers or gurus. Someone said to me once how discouraging it is when leading a Bible study to be asked, 'What do you want me to answer?', as if the whole process is a kind of gradual striptease of revelation by the omniscient leader who gradually takes the clothes off the passage to reveal the heart of the text to the waiting group.

A prayerful dependence upon the Spirit is bound to affect the way we preach and teach. There will be about our preaching something of the spirit of one who has been listening and who is praying as he preaches. There will be an earnestness and passion. We will be doing much more than just a cold explaining of the Bible text. But we must not mistake an apparently passionate style with the ministry of the Spirit. For the Spirit is sovereign. We cannot enlist His support by preaching in a particular style, just as we cannot guarantee His work in our hearts by listening with a particular technique or in a particular place or manner. He blows where and when He wills and we cannot constrain Him. Our prayer is not a kind of magic wand to bring the Spirit. Magic, after all, is a way of using supernatural power with me in charge; I wave the wand. But I am never in charge of the Spirit. Our prayer is to be a genuine expression of heartfelt and utter dependence upon Him to work, for until and unless He opens blind eyes and softens hard hearts, the Father will not be made known. Charles Spurgeon used to advise his students to prepare as though it all depended upon them, and then to do what he did as he ascended the pulpit steps, saying under his breath the words, 'I believe in the Holy Spirit, the Lord, the Giver of Life.'

We should thank God for the testimony of the Spirit to Jesus. We should pray daily and urgently for His work of bringing deep conviction in our own hearts and the hearts of others, conviction of our sin, conviction of Christ's righteousness and conviction of the devil's judgement. We must thank God for His ministry, leading and guiding us to walk in the way of apostolic and biblical truth, praying that He would shine His light on the page, open our blind eyes, and move our hearts to desire what we ought to desire and hate the evil we ought to hate. We thank Him for His gracious anointing of all believers and the way that anointing helps us to recognise error. And we should pray that His equipping ministry will enable us to play our part in bringing the declaration of gospel forgiveness to many people. We need to pray that He will make the Father known to us deeply, so that the truths we affirm feel to us both true and real in experience. And we should pray that He will work in us the virtues of honesty about ourselves, an openness to God's truth in Scripture, a humble acknowledgement of the role my Christian brothers and sisters play in helping me understand and obey the Bible, a hard-working attentiveness to Scripture and, above all, a steady life-changing obedience. For this is His aim.

When frustrated by powerlessness in ministry, we turn neither to mysticism nor to bare history. Rather, we return again and again to the Bible, crying out in prayer that the Spirit will bear witness to hearts, wills, minds and consciences through that historical witness.

So when I feel dry in my Christian life, I will not turn away from the Bible to some parallel and alternative place of revelation. I will not lazily hope to read my Bible and get some mystical and painless meaning from it. No, I will renew my zeal to listen to the Bible, praying more and more that the Spirit will graciously work in me His wonderful work of conviction, so that my heart is warmed, my mind instructed and my will moved to align itself with God's will. Above all, I will cry out in prayer that by the ministry of the Spirit through the Bible, Jesus will continue to make the Father known to me and to others through me. May God burden us to do that, to the honour and glory of Jesus.

Bibliography

COMMENTARIES ON JOHN'S GOSPEL

C.K. Barrett, *The Gospel according to St. John* (2nd Edition. London: SPCK, 1978)

Gary M. Burge, *John* (Grand Rapids, Michigan: Zondervan NIV Application Commentary, 2002)

D.A. Carson, *The Gospel according to John* (Leicester: IVP, 1991)

John Chrysostom, *Homilies on the Gospel of St. John* (Peabody, Massachusetts: Zondervan, 'Nicene and Post-Nicene Fathers' Vol. 14, 2004)

Andreas Köstenberger, *John* (Grand Rapids, Michigan: Baker Exegetical Commentary, 2004)

Dick Lucas and William Philip, *Teaching John* (Ross-shire: Christian Focus/PT Media, 2002)

Leon Morris, *The Gospel according to John* (Revised Edition) (Grand Rapids, Michigan: Eerdmans New International Commentary on the New Testament, 1995)

Lesslie Newbigin, *The Light has Come* (Grand Rapids, Michigan: Eerdmans, 1982)

William Temple, *Readings in St.John's Gospel* (London: Macmillan, 1961)

OTHER BOOKS AND ARTICLES

Peter Adam, *Hearing God's Words* (New Studies in Biblical Theology. Leicester: IVP/Apollos, 2004)

Peter Adam, *Written for Us* (Nottingham: IVP, 2008)

J.L. Austin, *How to do things with words* (2nd Edition, Cambridge, Massachusetts: Harvard University Press, 1975)

Rob Bell, *Love Wins*, (San Francisco: Collins, 2011)

Rob Bell, *Velvet Elvis* (Grand Rapids, Michigan: Zondervan, 2005)

Ellis R. Brotzman, *Old Testament Textual Criticism* (Grand Rapids, Michigan: Baker, 1994)

Jack Deere, *Surprised by the Voice of God* (Grand Rapids, Michigan: Zondervan, 2006)

Jonathan Edwards, 'A Narrative of Surprising Conversions' in *Jonathan Edwards on Revival* (Edinburgh: Banner of Truth, 1991)

John M. Frame, 'The Spirit and the Scriptures' in D.A. Carson and John D. Woodbridge (eds), *Hermeneutics, Authority and Canon* (Leicester: IVP, 1986)

Hans Frei, *The Eclipse of Biblical Narrative. A Study in Eighteenth and Nineteenth Century Hermeneutics* (New Haven: Yale University Press, 1974)

Graeme Goldsworthy, *Gospel-centred Hermeneutics* (Nottingham: IVP/Apollos, 2006)

Wayne Grudem, *The Gift of Prophecy in the New Testament and Today* (Wheaton, Illinois: Crossway, 2000)

William Hague *William Wilberforce* (London: HarperCollins 2007)

Bibliography

C.E. Hill, *Who Chose the Gospels? Probing the Great Gospel Conspiracy* (Oxford: Oxford University Press, 2010)

Christopher Hitchens, *God is not great* (London: Atlantic Books, 2007)

Peter Hitchens, *The Rage against God* (London: Continuum, 2010)

Joyce Huggett, *Listening to God* (2nd Edition, London: Hodder & Stoughton, 1996)

David Jackman, *Spirit of Truth* (Ross-shire: Christian Focus/PT Media, 2006)

Andreas Köstenberger and Scott R. Swain, *Father, Son and Spirit: The Trinity and John's Gospel* (Nottingham: IVP/Apollos, 2008)

C.S. Lewis, *An Experiment in Criticism* (Cambridge: Cambridge University Press, 1961)

D.M. Lloyd-Jones, *Preaching and Preachers* (London: Hodder and Stoughton, 1971)

D.M. Lloyd-Jones, *Authority* (London: Inter-Varsity Fellowship, 1958)

Martin Luther, *The Bondage of the Will* (translated J.I. Packer and O.R. Johnston. London: James Clarke, 1957)

Brian McLaren, *A New Kind of Christianity* (London: Hodder & Stoughton, 2010)

J. Gresham Machen, *Christianity and Liberalism* (new edition. Grand Rapids, Michigan: Eerdmans, 2009)

I. Howard Marshall, *Beyond the Bible: moving from Scripture to Theology* (Grand Rapids, Michigan: Baker, 2004)

Bruce M. Metzger, *A Textual Commentary on the Greek New Testament* (3rd Edition. Stuttgart, United Bible Societies, 1975)

Robert Morgan, with John Barton, *Biblical Interpretation* (Oxford: Oxford University Press, 1988)

Jonathan Mumme, 'The Spirit, the Spirits, and the Letter: Martin Luther on the Holy Spirit and the Holy Scriptures' in *Modern Reformation,* November 2010, pp. 18-22

Iain Murray, *The Old Evangelicalism* (Edinburgh: Banner of Truth, 2005)

John Owen, *Communion with the Triune God* (Kelly M. Kapic and Justin Taylor (eds)) (Wheaton, Illinois: Crossway, 2007)

J.I. Packer, *Knowing God* (London: Hodder and Stoughton, 1973)

John Piper, *Tested by Fire* (Leicester: IVP, 2001)

Philip Pullman, *The good man Jesus and the scoundrel Christ* (London: Canongate, 2010)

Michael Raiter, *Stirrings of the Soul: Evangelicals and the New Spirituality* (London: Good Book Company, 2003)

Peter Sanlon, 'Depth and Weight: Augustine's Sermon Illustration' in *Churchman* 122/1 (Church Society, Watford) (Spring 2008), pp. 61-75

Janet Soskice, *Sisters of Sinai* (London: Chatto and Windus, 2009)

George Steiner, *Real Presences* (Chicago: University of Chicago Press, 1989)

Mark Stibbe, *John's Gospel* (London: Routledge, 1994)

John R.W. Stott, *I believe in Preaching* (London: Hodder and Stoughton, 1982)

Timothy C.F. Stunt, *From Awakening to Secession: Radical Evangelicals in Switzerland and Britain 1815-1835* (Edinburgh: T & T Clark, 2000)

Helmut Thielicke, *The Prayer that Spans the World: sermons on the Lord's Prayer* (ET London: James Clarke, 1965)

A.C. Thiselton, *New Horizons in Hermeneutics* (London: HarperCollins, 1992)

Bibliography

Mark D. Thompson, *A Clear and Present Word* (New Studies in Biblical Theology. Nottingham: IVP/Apollos, 2006)

Daniel J. Trier and David Lauber (eds), *Trinitarian Theology for the Church* (Nottingham: IVP/Apollos, 2009)

Kevin J.Vanhoozer, *Is there a meaning in this text?* (Leicester: IVP/Apollos, 1998)

Kevin J. Vanhoozer, *First Theology* (Nottingham: IVP/Apollos, 2002)

Kevin J. Vanhoozer, *The Drama of Doctrine* (Louisville, Kentucky: Westminster John Knox Press, 2005)

Kevin J. Vanhoozer, 'Triune Discourse' in *Trinitarian Theology for the Church* (Daniel J. Trier and David Lauber (eds)) (Nottingham: IVP/Apollos, 2009)

Timothy Ward, *Words of Life* (Nottingham: IVP, 2009)

Keith Warrington, *The Message of the Holy Spirit* (Bible Speaks Today. Nottingham: IVP, 2009)

David F. Wells, *God the Evangelist* (Exeter: Paternoster, 1987)

David F. Wells, *The Courage to be Protestant* (Nottingham: IVP, 2008)

John Wenham, *Christ and the Bible* (Guildford, Surrey: Eagle, 1993)

John Woodhouse, 'The preacher and the living Word' in Christopher Green and David Jackman (eds), *When God's Voice is Heard* (2nd Edition, Leicester: IVP, 2003)

Telford Work, *Living and Active: Scripture in the Economy of Salvation* (Grand Rapids, Michigan: Eerdmans, 2002)

N.T. Wright, *The New Testament and the People of God* (London: SPCK, 1992)

N.T. Wright, *The Last Word: Beyond the Bible Wars to a New Understanding of the Authority of Scripture* (San Francisco: HarperCollins, 2005), published in the UK as *Scripture and the Authority of God* (London: SPCK, 2005)

Acknowledgments

This book began with two addresses on 'The Word and the Spirit in John's Gospel' given at the Evangelical Ministry Assembly in London in June 2010. I am grateful to Vaughan Roberts and the Proclamation Trust for the invitation to speak. I have also been helped by the students on the PT Cornhill Training Course who asked thoughtful questions when I inflicted some inchoate versions of this material on them.

Five colleagues and friends worked carefully through the draft manuscript and kindly gave me many challenging and perceptive comments: David Jackman, Dick Lucas, Paul Perkin, Adrian Reynolds and John Woodhouse. The end result is much the better for their help, although of course the final version is my own responsibility. I am also grateful to Sam Parkinson for editorial assistance and Nikki Tomkins for secretarial help. I am, as always, deeply grateful to my wife Carolyn for her patient encouragement and loving support.

PT RESOURCES

RESOURCES FOR PREACHERS AND BIBLE TEACHERS

PT Resources, a ministry of The Proclamation Trust, provides a range of multimedia resources for preachers and Bible teachers.

Teach the Bible Series (Christian Focus & PT Resources)
The Teaching the Bible Series, published jointly with Christian Focus Publications, is written by preachers, for preachers, and is specifically geared to the purpose of God's Word – its proclamation as living truth. Books in the series aim to help the reader move beyond simply understanding a text to communicating and applying it.

Current titles include: *Teaching Numbers, Teaching Isaiah, Teaching Amos, Teaching Matthew, Teaching John, Teaching Acts, Teaching Romans, Teaching Ephesians, Teaching 1 and 2 Thessalonians, Teaching 1 Timothy, Teaching 2 Timothy, Teaching 1 Peter, Teaching the Christian Hope.*

PT Resources, a ministry of The Proclamation Trust, provides a range of multimedia resources for preachers and Bible teachers.

Teach the Bible Series (Christian Focus & PT Resources)
The Teaching the Bible Series, published jointly with Christian Focus Publications, is written by preachers, for preachers, and is specifically geared to the purpose of God's Word – its proclamation as living truth. Books in the series aim to help the reader move beyond simply understanding a text to communicating and applying it.

Current titles include: *Teaching Numbers, Teaching Isaiah, Teaching Amos, Teaching Matthew, Teaching John, Teaching Acts, Teaching Romans, Teaching Ephesians, Teaching 1 and 2 Thessalonians, Teaching 1 Timothy, Teaching 2 Timothy, Teaching 1 Peter, Teaching the Christian Hope.*

Practical Preacher series
PT Resources publish a number of books addressing practical issues for preachers. These include *The Priority of Preaching, Bible Delight, Hearing the Spirit, The Ministry Medical, Burning Hearts* and *Spirit of Truth.*

Online resources
We publish a large number of audio resources online, all of which are free to download. These are searchable through our website by speaker, date, topic and Bible book. The resources include:

- sermon series; examples of great preaching which not only demonstrate faithful principles, but which will refresh and encourage the heart of the preacher

- instructions; audio which helps the teacher or preacher understand, open up and teach individual books of the Bible by getting to grips with their central message and purpose

- conference recordings; audio from all our conferences including the annual Evangelical Ministry Assembly. These talks discuss ministry and preaching issues.

An increasing number of resources are also available in video download form.

Online DVD

PT Resources have recently published online our collection of instructional videos by David Jackman. This material has been taught over the past 20 years on our PT Cornhill training course and around the world. It gives step-by-step instructions on handling each genre of biblical literature. There is also an online workbook. The videos are suitable for preachers and those teaching the Bible in a variety of different contexts. Access to all the videos is free of charge.

The Proclaimer

Visit the Proclaimer blog for regular updates on matters to do with preaching. This is a short, punchy blog refreshed daily, which is written by preachers and for preachers. It can be accessed via the PT website or through:

www.theproclaimer.org.uk.

TRUTHFORLIFE®

THE BIBLE-TEACHING MINISTRY OF **ALISTAIR BEGG**

The mission of Truth For Life is to teach the Bible with clarity and relevance so that unbelievers will be converted, believers will be established, and local churches will be strengthened.

Daily Program

Each day, Truth For Life distributes the Bible teaching of Alistair Begg across the U.S., in selected cities in Canada, and in several locations outside of the U.S. on over 1,700 radio outlets. To find a radio station near you, visit *truthforlife.org/station-finder.*

Free Teaching

The daily program, and Truth For Life's entire teaching archive of over 2,000 Bible-teaching messages, can be accessed for free online and through Truth For Life's full-feature mobile app. A daily app is also available that provides direct access to the daily message and daily devotional. Download the free mobile apps at *truthforlife.org/app* and listen free online at *truthforlife.org.*

At-Cost Resources

Books and full-length teaching from Alistair Begg on CD, DVD and MP3CD are available for purchase *at cost, with no mark up.* Visit *truthforlife.org/store.*

Where To Begin?

If you're new to Truth For Life and would like to know where to begin listening and learning, find starting point suggestions at *truthforlife.org/firststep.* For a full list of ways to connect with Truth For Life, visit *truthforlife.org/subscribe.*

Contact Truth For Life

P.O. Box 398000 Cleveland, Ohio 44139

phone 1 (888) 588-7884   **email** letters@truthforlife.org

 /truthforlife   @truthforlife truthforlife.org